To Lau[illegible]

Wishing you
Peace & Joy
on your
JOURNEY

Love in Christ
Connie

When You Miss the Rainbow

Connie Teilborg

AmeriPress
Phoenix, Arizona

Scripture verses at the beginning of each chapter are the author's paraphrase.

In some instances names have been changed to protect anonymity.

Library of Congress Catalog Card Number: 96-86819

ISBN: 0-9640421-7-7

Cover design: Terry Harper

Published in the United States by
AMERIPRESS
3420 East Shea Blvd., Suite 235
Phoenix, Arizona 85028

Manufactured in the United States of America

10 9 8 7 6 5 4 3 2 1

Dedicated to the two who said

"Please write a book about your experience. Your journey was not for you alone!"

Florence Littauer
&
Dr. Carl Hammerschlag

Table of Contents

FOREWORD

When I learned about Connie Teilborg's massive overdose of estrogen and subsequent disorientation, I was appalled, of course. I felt confident, though, that after certain medical countermeasures (antidotes) and some appropriate counseling, she would snap back to her usual organized, confident self.... Well, I was wrong.

Even though I have spent thirty years teaching, speaking, writing, and counseling all over the world, I had underestimated the depth of despair into which my friend would drop. She never even told me what had happened. Connie has always been able to rise above adverse circumstances. She could line up her own ducks—and those of everyone else!—in straight rows. Connie's carefully crafted coping mechanisms ultimately failed her.

When You Miss the Rainbow recounts the process entailed in conquering depression. Connie Teilborg skillfully blends both her own story and much important information that everyone needs to know. The dialogue is snappy, the descriptions graphic. This book is a real page-turner.

You'll want to read and reread certain portions. Allow time for the significant concepts to penetrate your heart and mind. Remind yourself that there's no quick fix for many of life's hurts. Face the fact that it's not noble to suffer in silence. Appreciate that God understands your need to vent, to purge yourself of past hostilities...that He is not the author of fear.

Many years ago, when I lost my two sons, when I faced circumstances I couldn't control, God gradually and graciously taught me that even though life is sometimes three steps forward and two steps back, the journey can be precious. I pray that you, too, can view the rainbow through your rain; that you will come to see life in wholly new ways.

Treasure *When You Miss the Rainbow*. You'll find hope and joy in your journey...and yes, you'll discover gold if you look in the right places.

Florence Littauer, President
Christian Leaders, Authors & Speakers Services

PROLOGUE

The eerily lit numbers from the nightstand clock lodged in my head: 4:16 AM. I stumbled out of bed, frantically fumbled for the bathroom light, and stared at the image in the mirror. Whose eyes were those looking back at me? Everything was bizarrely distorted, surreal. "Please God, what's happening to me?" I cried. I was breaking up! My body and mind were shattering into confetti and scattering everywhere. I was terrified!

I am crazy! screamed my brain to the rest of me. *I am really, absolutely, positively crazy. I will have to die. Somehow, someway, I will have to die!* I staggered my way back into bed, my body shaking uncontrollably. My husband, Jim, was jarred out of his sound sleep. He desperately tried to find out what had happened to me in a period of just a few hours.

Jim called the gynecologist immediately. She told us to alert our family doctor. He'd meet us without delay at his office. Terrified and trembling, I was sitting on his examining table as he walked in with my file in his hand. Shaking his head, he said in bewilderment, "I just finished talking with your gynecologist, Connie, and I'm so sorry to have to tell you a tragic mistake has been made!"

My nightmare had only begun. A lab error involving transposed numbers had led to my being administered a massive dose of estrogen. Following a hysterectomy, treatment—that should have been routine—thrust me into a long period of agitation and anxiety coupled with deep depression.

The Unresolved Issues

Several months into my attempts to regain some equilibrium in my life, a Phoenix medical doctor attuned to a holistic approach gently suggested that my problems might be more complex than the toxic dose of estrogen. This doctor recognizes that mind, body, and spirit are all intertwined in the healing process. I believe he really understood my heart and my frustration with the turtle pace of my particular healing. This wise man steered me to Tucson to see a Harvard-trained physician, Dr. Andrew Weil, highly schooled in integrative medicine.

I allowed myself to feel a bit hopeful. The astute doctor asked many probing questions, most of which I'd not encountered during a medical examination.

"What was it like for you growing up? What kind of relationship do you have with your husband, children, parents? What about your diet? Do you exercise? What kind and how much? What do you do for recreation?"

He closed our interview with this observation: "I've not heard of anyone being injected with such massive doses of estrogen. Most certainly that would throw your body out of kilter and disrupt the neurotransmitters in your brain. I believe, however, there is a great deal more to your depression than an overdose of medicine. It could be that the mishap uncovered other trauma. My sense is you may have unresolved issues in your life. I would like for you to see my friend and colleague, Dr. Carl Hammerschlag, when you return to Phoenix. I believe he will be able to help you. For now, you must make yourself exercise at least thirty minutes twice a day to stimulate the endorphines in your brain. This should ease the depression."

Good grief! I had worked diligently to control my life. What was Dr. Weil talking about? Did he think the overdose was the proverbial straw? Was it the sudden power surge that blew the circuit? I, like many others, was reluctant to uncover any unpleasant truths about myself.

But should I investigate? Getting one more medical person involved in this process didn't much appeal to me. I was barely able to keep my head above water. Perhaps I had no choice; I had to do more than merely hang on by a tenuous thread.

I made an appointment to see Dr. Hammerschlag the following week.

Introduction: The Rainbow

INTRODUCTION
The Rainbow

Genesis 9:16 *Whenever I see a rainbow in the sky, I will remember the abiding promises God has made to me.*

Missing The Rainbow

It wasn't till much later that an insight crystallized what I had been learning during the years of my therapy. Synchronized with a flash of lightning, it came to me. Driving to our vacation home in Greer, in the beautiful White Mountains of Arizona, I rounded the bend near the Sunrise Ski Area. The torrential downpour that had followed me from Pinetop abated into a slight drizzle. Just ahead and off to the right appeared the most exquisite rainbow! Each color was distinctly defined and brilliant. This extraordinary gift seemed to originate from behind the highest peak and descend into the thickest pines. Completing this picture was an old corral nestled in the meadow area. This glorious sight took my breath away; my eyes brimmed with tears at the spectacular beauty of God's creation.

But I knew at that instant I had missed the rainbow. I'd been so focused on seizing the pot of gold that I had bypassed the joy of the journey. I hadn't even **seen** the rainbow! Perhaps, sadly, that has been your experience, too. In my case, for nearly fifty years I'd yielded to the temptation to do almost anything to escape the painful parts of life. I had hurried, maneuvered, manipulated, cajoled, railed—whatever it took—to stretch for that elusive gold. I'd become a human "doing" instead of a human "being."

> **The rainbow, of course, is an arch of brilliant colors that appears in the sky when the sun shines after a shower of rain. It is formed in the part of the sky opposite the sun. Red, orange, yellow, green, blue, indigo, and violet are the seven colors in the rainbow. Seven is the perfect number in the Bible; one day it occurred to me that God allocated to the rainbow the perfect number of colors. I believe He created the rainbow resplendent and magnificent to remind us His ways are flawless. Why, then, had it taken me so long to relinquish control of my life to God and to accept this truth?**

Blending the Colors

The experienced rainbow observer sees a subtle blending of the colors and doesn't feel threatened if each color is not clearly defined. I'd missed much of this beautiful merging because I had refused to take time to listen to God's gentle whispers.

The width of each band of color in the rainbow depends upon the size of the raindrops. When the raindrops came into my life and were a consistent size, something I could anticipate, I felt secure. I could manage a few little problems. During those times the colors were distinct and separate, and I could see clearly the path in front of me. Each color occupied the "right" amount of space, not too much—nor too little. At other times, when the colors of my life displayed different, unusual proportions, I'd become anxious and bewildered. That's when I panicked and took things into my own hands.

Comprehending these not-so-predictable experiences as part of the Master's plan was difficult for me. I knew little of going with the flow, of allowing the colors to blend or to take up different-sized spaces. Delighting in the beauty of the irregularity, the spontaneity, was lost on me. How could I wait for God to define the size and shades of the colors of my life? What if He didn't do *what* I wanted Him to do? What if He didn't do it *the way* I wanted Him to do it? And, what if He didn't do it *in my timing*? Such stubborn pride. Such gall!

I learned every rainbow is a complete circle. The circle cannot be observed from the ground; it can be viewed from the sky, however. That appealed to me! I wanted, and believed I needed, to see the complete circle. Playing god in my life was intriguing, and I ignored the truth that **only** God sees the whole circle as I witness just part of the arc.

Our eyes view a rainbow when the sun is behind us and the rain in front. But I wanted to see the sun ahead. Desiring the sun to be in front—the things we perceive as good things—is natural. And, oh, how I wanted the rain far, far behind. I'd run as fast as I could to leave the pain and darkness in the distance. I was terrified of resting in the pain and learning what God wanted to teach me.

It was alien to me to completely trust Him with what I needed to know for my spiritual and emotional growth. In the last few years, I've come to understand that seeing the rainbow is not possible until I'm willing to look into the rain, to walk in the rain, to wait in the rain, and to rest in the rain, trusting all the while that the Master's plan is at work in my life.

Telling My Story

Driving that day in the rain shower I knew, with all my heart, that I was to tell you my story. Perhaps, in the sharing of my story, I can give you hope when your rain is ahead and your sun behind. Perhaps I can offer you comfort and reassurance that your pain, too, will pass.

In the rainbow, symbolizing the journey, are lessons you can't or won't learn any other way. I pray you can believe that these life-changing lessons can nourish your soul, strengthen your heart, and bless the lives you touch.

If you've missed the rainbow, it's not too late. The pot of gold can wait.

CHAPTER ONE
The Black Storm

Job 3:25-26 *The thing I feared most has come to pass; the dreaded event has happened. I am empty of tranquility and filled with anxiety. My soul finds no rest.*

Black does not appear in God's rainbow . . . for black is the absence of light. Black is the color of depression. "Blue" days come upon most people occasionally and pass quickly: nothing to be alarmed about. But, oh, how different loom the black days! And clinical depression represents the blackest of the black: the storm at its worst.

Just when it appears that light and hope might tentatively emerge from the dark clouds of despair, the storm intensifies. The sky threatens. The clouds multiply, enlarge, and darken. They suppress any hint that life might be worth living again—ever!

The blackness of depression is lightless, lifeless, desolate, hopeless.

Splotches of Blackness

When did the blackness in my life begin? Perhaps it started when Dr. Barber, our family doctor for many years, told my mother she was pregnant with her second child.

"What! It can't be. I cannot have another baby, not

now." Already overwhelmed by circumstances, this mother felt it was all too much. The eldest of eight, Lucile had spent her childhood and adolescence tightly controlled by her minister father, misunderstood by her delicate mother, and charged with much of the care of her younger brothers and sisters. The family was poor; the children wore hand-me-downs from the parishioners. Mom had hoped for more security when she married.

But now Lucile was living in cramped quarters on farmland with her husband, nine-month-old son, mother-in-law, and several of her husband's siblings. She could not bear the idea of more entrapment. I would be another rock to tie to this perilously close-to-sinking person drowning from the lack of privacy and feelings of utter helplessness and dependency.

"Isn't there somewhere you could go?" volunteered Dr. Barber, "perhaps a building on the farm that you could make livable?" Ultimately, that's what happened. Lumber was gathered from the site of an old fallen-down house on the desolate prairie; the dwelling was pieced together and erected in the same yard as my grandmother's home. Over the years Mother would constantly remind us that we didn't have a "real" house. Things weren't as they should be. Mother would always have to make do.

And so this infant, Constance Anderson, was brought home from the hospital to that house. The tale of the unplanned child became a repetitive theme. Not only was I an "accident," I was also a burdensome live-wire. Mother made special note of this fact in my baby book. The story brightened, though, when Mother became pregnant with my sister, Vicki. "Vicki is our only child who was planned," Mother often announced.

My baby book continued to be a sad revelation. Mother put these words into my mouth after my first year picture: "My mother made me a cake with a green candle on it. *But I didn't even get to taste it!* Mother didn't have enough film in her camera to take a picture of me. She did take this picture of me later. I have on the dress Grandma Anderson gave me for my birthday." And next to my second birthday picture: "We were too busy at this time of year to celebrate. We did have cake and ice cream with the folks at the other house. My mother taught school last year and will this year, too!" One might think this baby book was about Mother rather than Little Connie.

Messages my mother gave to me as a child ring in my brain: "What a handful you are! When your brother was your age, he just sat where he was put. But you're all over the place, never still a minute. Why are you **always** where you're not supposed to be? Why can't you just sit? Stop skipping in the house. Stop! Stop!! Stop!!!" I was naughty. I was disobedient. I was a disappointment. And I was filled with shame!

One day when Grandmother Jaeger came to visit,

Mother locked me out of the house. The reason remains fuzzy, but I distinctly remember my grandmother being horrified. "Lucile, you mustn't lock your child out of her own home."

"I just can't stand to have her around!" Mother shot back.

The Worsening Storm

And the spankings, oh, those innumerable spankings. First, Mom tried yardsticks. Those broke. Next, I graduated to rulers. Those broke, too. Finally, she found the perfect tool: a black, steel ruler. It was an ideal choice because no matter how many times she spanked me or how hard, the black ruler never broke! It was indestructible. Not at all like my spirit.

Mom took me to the cellar for the spankings—far away from others' eyes and ears. The tiny space under our house was dark and dank and loaded with spiders. They seemed all the more menacing because of the environment. I remember thinking, *This must be how prisoners have to live—in a little, cold, dark cell just like this.* Sometimes I felt like one of those prisoners.

My fear of spiders was intensified during my fifth summer. My brother, Kennie, and I were visiting my mother's parents. Grandmother Jaeger was a kindly soul and Grandfather Jaeger was very stern and rigid. My treasured birthday present from my Grandma Jaeger was a doll that said, "Ma-Ma" when she was turned over on her tummy. In the kitchen with Grandmother and Kennie looking on, I showed off my dolly. All of a sudden the kitchen door burst open, and there, framed in the doorway, was my furiously angry, red-faced grandfather.

"If you make that doll say, 'Ma-Ma' one more time, you're going to be in serious trouble!" For the life of me, I could not figure out why my doll shouldn't do what she was created to do. As soon as Grandpa left, I turned her over. With the "Ma-Ma" barely out of the doll's mouth, through the door burst Grandfather. He ripped the doll away from me, grabbed me tightly by the arm and admonished, "Down to the basement you go, and you'll stay there all night!"

"Oh, no!" implored my brother. "She's really afraid of basements and she hates spiders!" Grandfather, undaunted by my brother's plea and my grandmother's admonition not to do this cruel deed, whisked me down the steps and tossed me into a scary, dingy room. Then, with much fanfare, he locked the door.

To say I was terrified was a monumental understatement. I spent the night huddled in a tiny ball all the while believing gigantic, black spiders would come at any moment. After that experience, I had terrible "spider nightmares" for years.

The Ill-fitting Puzzle

How much of this blackness does a little girl's spirit

absorb? No one knows for certain. I imagine it's different for everybody. What I do know is that all the pieces come together to make up our wholeness. These pieces of my life's puzzle seem like jagged edges: sharp and cutting and cruel. They speak volumes about my former inability to feel loved, nourished, and cherished.

Affirming Love

It is critical for a child to have a secure foundation of invariable, affirming love. When he or she is deprived of it, the groundwork is laid for physical and emotional disorders. Basic needs are not met so the child must devise ways to receive attention—methods which are inappropriate and often involve obsessive-compulsive behavior in one form or other.

Mine involved trying harder to do more in order to become better. At the very least, I believed I had to do ten times more than anyone else just to be considered "even."

Neither Good Nor Pretty

Mother traveled for her sorority one summer when I was quite young. She left me in charge of meals and cleaning. I loved it! It was fun playing house and there weren't any angry words to spoil the fantasy. I was determined to have the whole place **perfect** when Mom got home. I spit and polished everything in sight. I even washed all the crystal on the topmost shelf, dusty from not being used. I thought Mom would be delighted when she returned home. She made little comment except to be disquieted when she found out I'd washed the crystal.

"What if you'd broken something?" was her reaction. I was crestfallen! Ashamed. I was never good enough. Nor, apparently, would I be considered pretty.

When I was twelve years old, a high school friend of my mother's came to visit. Like many girls that age I was especially vulnerable. I felt dreadfully skinny and ugly, neither child nor adult. Everything was magnified, primarily the things I deemed negative about myself.

I was in the bedroom and overheard my mother's friend say, "Connie is turning out to be such a pretty girl and so sweet, too."

Mom replied, "Oh, no! I don't think she'll ever be pretty. I do hope I can teach her to fix herself up so at least she'll be somewhat attractive."

Mother didn't intend for me to hear her comments, but, nevertheless, I did. The damage was done. Before this incident, I believed all mothers thought their daughters were pretty.

Blunt Talk

Reflecting on this episode, I am reminded of the times I have been blunt about my sons to a friend. My remarks may have been hurtful to Andy and Jay had they heard them; a reminder to us as parents to be watchful and sensitive to our children's emotions.

When I started high school, Mom was concerned whether I'd fit in because I'd attended a tiny, three-room, country grade school. The high school wasn't large, about 200 students. To me, however, it loomed huge. Mom was teaching junior high English so we rode to and from school together. One afternoon as we were driving home, Mother stated in a matter-of-fact manner, " I don't think it's such a good idea for you to spend so much time around Sally and Julie. They're much prettier than you and they make you look unattractive. Why don't you cultivate Mary as a friend? She's a nice girl, but she's not pretty. Then, compared to her, you'd look more appealing." No doubt my mother's observation was intended to be helpful, but it devastated me. It confirmed what I already believed about myself: neither good nor pretty.

77 to 1

Curious, isn't it, the things we remember? A psychologist friend believes we should hear 77 positive things to make up for one negative comment. Perhaps the numbers are a bit arbitrary, but I do believe the black things stick with us. They work their way from our consciousness into our subconsciousness where they stay to churn and

boil. They need to be excised or they can—and will—do unthinkable damage to our minds, bodies, and spirits.

An isolated, stormy incident in my childhood, or in yours, may not appear to particularly harm a child. And yes, some children are more resilient than others. But the cumulative effect of the multiplied cruel looks and comments, the heavy spankings meted out in anger, the lack of nurturing, is damage to a precious human being.

A Better Place

My coping mechanisms became fine-tuned during those growing up years. I learned to go to a different place, a special spot in my heart where I would be safe. This extraordinary place was a pretty white house with red geraniums in the window boxes. The soft green lawn was shaded with lots of lovely, big trees. I sat outside on the grass with my "real" family, a family who spoke in muted tones to one another always with love and respect. They played together and worked together peacefully. They respected one another. They were my hidden link to a safe world—a world where Little Connie was loved and accepted for who she was, not for what she was or what she did.

In this make-believe family we had our meals on time. This was an obvious sore spot between my mother and father. Because Dad farmed and fed cattle, his schedule varied. Many a screeching match took place when my father was late for breakfast or lunch or dinner. Mealtime became a time of horror for me. Would we eat our meals in peace or would war erupt? I remember waking up in the mornings to the sounds of Mom and Dad yelling at one another. Many times I was so nauseated that I could not eat. I tended to sympathize with Dad. I know how hard he worked, and I believe he tried to get in on time.

Spirits Healed

All too many adult kids find it difficult to recall happy, relaxed meals; vacations that were fun; parents who showed in a variety of ways they cared for one another and their offspring. But they do remember houses filled with foreboding. They tense up thinking about the constant watchfulness required to keep one step ahead of the next menacing event.

My experience is just one among thousands, maybe millions. Yet we wounded children must recognize that until our spirits are healed, we cannot be at peace. More than two thousand years ago, Plato wrote, "If the head and body are to be well, you must begin with the soul; that is the first thing." Such awareness is critical to our becoming flourishing, well-integrated individuals.

Parents' Pain Passed On

Maybe my parents did the best they knew to do. Perhaps they had no way of understanding my fragile spirit. They were dealing with their own unresolved issues and pain when I arrived on the scene.

Today, I believe my foundation for clinical depression was cemented into place during those early years. Many who suffer from depression are those keenly aware of the disapproval and rejection of others. I had an insatiable need to please, to be thought of positively, and to be loved and accepted. I was well on my way to becoming a **perfectionist**.

There's a story told about the lady standing on the street corner with her enormous, cardboard sign. Her message states in bold, black letters: **WILL WORK FOR APPROVAL!** That could have been me.

Even as a little girl, was I depression waiting to happen?

CHAPTER TWO
Little Red Hen

Jeremiah 29:11 *I have awesome plans to bless you. My blueprint will brighten your days with hope.*

One person traveling through the rainbow of life might well enjoy the vividness—the vitality—of red, the first gorgeous band. She would appreciate the excitement of wondering how this color would shade into the rest. For me, though, red was an alarm: a signal that I'd better stop and make a plan. I, for many years, was like that feisty, well-known creature in folklore: Little Red Hen.

Remember the story of this enterprising chicken? She found a grain of wheat and she decided to do something constructive with it. She would plant it and she, most assuredly, would need some assistance.

Red Hen questions Dog who was passing by on his morning walk. Would he like to help? He's busy walking, so he declines. Next, Red Hen sees Cat resting on the haystack. Cat is too sleepy to assist right then. Red Hen spots Pig who is sitting in a mud puddle washing his back. Not easily thwarted, she presents her plan to Pig. Nope, he's much too busy scrubbing to participate.

Poor Red Hen? Not necessarily. Dog had his own morning schedule. He was busy exercising when Red

Hen asked him to help. Maybe he was depressed. Perhaps he knew that exercising twice a day for thirty minutes would elevate the endorphines in his brain so he'd feel better. Dog might have accommodated Red Hen had she taken his schedule into consideration and allowed him to suggest a more convenient time to help her.

And what about Cat? It should have been obvious to Red Hen that Cat needed her sleep. Maybe Cat would have been willing to work after she was well rested.

And, for goodness sake, we all know that Pig seldom washed his back. When Pig declined to help Red Hen, he was undoubtedly doing himself, and the rest of the barnyard animals, a big favor by tidying-up.

Her Way Or Else

For Red Hen, it was either her way or no way. She had devised a plan and she was sticking to it. As far as she was concerned, there weren't **any** valid excuses for the other animals not participating. And that's the way it was with Red Hen.

I decided from my tumultuous, early experiences that I should always have a plan. I couldn't just let things happen—take their natural course—because the outcome might be something I hadn't anticipated. I wouldn't know how to respond, and I would find that frightening. So, I thought things out well in advance like Little Red Hen and included those people and things that fit into my design. When something happened to and around me that was out of my control, I was thrown for a loop.

Tripped Up By a Hose

My compulsion to plan ahead worked decidedly against me one fine day. I'd left the Phoenix summer heat behind and was delighting in the idea of several cool, calm, refreshing months in the mountains. I stopped at a self-serve gas station and put the nozzle in the tank. I contemplated that because I was so close to the nursery, I'd get some more of those pretty red geraniums I'd purchased a few days ago. Before I would do that, though, I'd go to the drug store. It was just around the corner—so no backtracking. "Just look at those filthy windows!" I muttered aloud. I put the gasoline nozzle on automatic, got the squeegee, some paper towels, and began to wash the windows. Hum, that reminded me that because I was going to the drug store, I'd better run over to Wal-Mart and pick up some paper towels. Should I do that after the nursery or before? Probably before, because I needed to stop at the grocery store, too.

All these plans were floating around in my head as I was washing the windows. I put the squeegee back and threw the towels away. I got into my car to pull up to the mini-market to pay and to get a paper. . . . My heavens, what was that? Why was my car jerking? What

was that strange noise?

"Oh, good grief!" Horrified, I discovered the nozzle of the gasoline hose was still in my tank as I was driving off. And the black hose was caught under the back tire. "What do I do now?" I screeched. I slammed the car in reverse. The hose stretched even tauter. Then it snapped! I thought my eyes were deceiving me. Surely this can't be happening! My heart pounded wildly as I blundered out of the car.

This busy station has many pumps and, yes, there was a vehicle at nearly every one: a Budweiser truck, a car with five teenagers, a motor home with an elderly couple. All eyes turned, at once, to stare at me. Worst of all, adjacent to where I had filled up were three cowboys in a pickup loaded with bales of hay. Decidedly, these were **not** gentlemen cowboys. Hurriedly, they trotted over to grab a look. All three began laughing hysterically, pounding one another on the back and generally having a jolly-good time.

In a flash, my mind took in all that was happening to and around me. I thought I was going to die from embarrassment. As stealthily as I could, I pulled the nozzle from the tank and tried my level best not to notice that, by this time, the cowboys were practically rolling on the ground with unmitigated glee. I took the nozzle, with the dangling bit of hose left attached, and walked to the station. Each step was agony. *Walk as nonchalantly as you can just as if this happens to you every day. Yes indeed, just another ordinary day, just another ordinary customer,* I told myself.

Obviously, this self-talk didn't work. I looked like a cat slinking along holding her broken tail. People inside were nose-to-glass, peering out to get a closer look at the commotion, and at the dimwit who had caused such an uproar.

The management attempted to soothe me. I was not the only fool, they encouraged. "Why, just the other day," one of the cashiers told me, "this guy pulls up in a big motor home. First of all, he hits number six pump. Then he backs into number three. And, if that's not bad enough, he's so flustered by this time that he rams number eight and practically knocks it over. So you see, you're not the only one."

But my humiliation was total; I felt horrible.

The black hose experience illustrates how I'd done much of my life. Instead of just taking care of the business at hand, I'd be planning my next step. I couldn't wait to move on to something else. That impatience had caused me much more than embarrassment. It had cost me the loss of the beauty in each moment, in each day, in the splendor of the rainbow.

Running the Universe

Although I had become a Christian when I was eleven, and had felt the comfort of a Heavenly Father watching over me, my faith was a bit skewed. I believed

God needed an assistant to help Him run the universe; God and I would do it together. I must confess, however, that often I craved someone with "skin on." I found managing the world, even with God's help, a mighty big job.

That's why I was a great fan of Little Red Hen. I could relate to her. She was industrious and she had a plan. Generous, she was willing to include others in her plan. When they didn't cooperate, she took punitive action by not allowing them any bread.

An Unsettled Feeling

So, like Red Hen, I thought God and I had the world in control—until the summer of 1991. Everything changed that infamous summer. It had been such a strange time. The searing desert heat seemed to be more offensive than in summers past. I hadn't been my usual self, nothing I could put my finger on, just an unsettling feeling that something was awry. A blood level estrogen test was ordered.

As the blood sample was being drawn, my concern mounted. I thought back to a routine physical at my gynecologist's office several years before. There was "thickening" that needed to be investigated. With my bladder nearly bursting with all the water I was required to drink for a clear picture, I tried to lie still enough to get a thorough reading from the ultrasound. Immediate surgery was scheduled. Ovarian cancer was mentioned and stuck in my mind like a barbed hook. The moments of dread the week before surgery were immeasurable. Signing the "do whatever you deem necessary" permission slip seemed a small price to pay to ferret out the problem. None too quickly, the day for surgery arrived.

Through the hazy fog of the residual anesthetic, I faintly heard my doctor say, "Good news, Connie, no cancer!" I later learned that endometriosis was the culprit and that everything in the area had been removed: uterus, ovaries, and appendix.

Had I been fully informed about my signed consent, I believe I would not have agreed to a complete hysterectomy without further understanding the ramifications of surgically induced menopause. Little did I realize this omission set the stage for what was to follow. A shot of estrogen was administered in the hospital, and my recovery appeared swift and sure.

Weighing ERT

A plan of ERT (estrogen replacement therapy) was discussed and a program using a small dose of Premarin each day was decided upon. I felt good and continued to "do" my life fairly much the way I always had—with determination, discipline, vigor, and, naturally, a plan.

Because I was so compliant in agreeing to a total hysterectomy, this same gynecologist offered me an opportunity to participate in an experimental drug study for the betterment of womankind. This study was to test the soon-to-be-released estrogen patches.

As the stereotypical people-pleaser, I was quick to agree. I was told I would be the ideal candidate, and that was music to my ears. It clinched the deal.

I began the study believing I was doing a lofty, noble thing. Caught up in the zeal of obliging, I had no way of discerning what havoc this study would wreak upon my body. I broke out in huge, red welts everywhere I placed a patch. Innumerable trips to the doctor's office, getting pills that might or might not contain estrogen, being subjected to devices that measured the extent of horrendous hot flashes, and a host of other disturbances, left me exhausted and discouraged. For the first time in my adult life, I felt I was losing my much relied-upon control. Trying to discontinue the study was not nearly as easy as agreeing to participate had been. I was scolded and implored, "See this through; finish what you've begun!"

The result? I abandoned my plan. At my final appointment with this doctor, I was admonished with this grim scenario: my bones would become brittle; I would break my hip, fall, and die of pneumonia—all because of my refusal to complete this study and/or take estrogen.

In actuality, I did fairly well for a couple of years without estrogen. But at this point, my new gynecologist suggested I start back on ERT because of the hot flashes and other uncomfortable symptoms I was beginning to experience.

The test results were astonishing. Despite the many pills and injections I'd been given, my body, amazingly, tested inordinately low in estrogen. An injection was ordered and given that same evening.

Out of Control

Within hours, extreme agitation nearly claimed me. I both feared death and began to long for it. Still sitting on the edge of the examining table, I vividly remember pleading with the doctor, "You have to help me. Please! I'm afraid I'm going to hurt myself."

He soberly responded, "We'll do our best to help you, Connie, we really, truly will."

The following weeks are a blurry haze. I went from one specialist to another, one drug to another. The goal was to attempt to reverse the damage the mammoth amount of estrogen had done to the neurotransmitters of my brain. I was poked, prodded, questioned, shuttled back and forth between doctors. I was completely powerless: my most terrifying fear!

Eventually, it was decided that nothing could be done to get rid of the estrogen. I would just have to weather the storm and wait for the estrogen to work itself out of my body. During this time, one of the specialists on the medical team treating me contacted the

Chief of Pharmacology of one of the major hospitals in the Phoenix area. He supported the theory that this toxic dose had catapulted me into severe depression. I was experiencing a deprivation of serotonin and/or norepinephrine, which are chemicals in the brain. The brain needs a balance of these chemicals in order to send appropriate messages to the rest of the body.

My affliction combined extreme anxiety with severe depression. It was especially disheartening trying to find effective medication. Some exaggerated the depression, others the anxiety. One drug after another was administered with hopes one would soon catch on and give me some reprieve from my agony. And, in most cases, it was necessary to wait two to three weeks before a new drug could be tried. As far as I was concerned, two to three weeks might well have been a million years.

Many days I could do nothing but stay curled up in the fetal position in my bed and pray to die. Some days I was able to get out of bed and brush my teeth, but do little else. The despair was indescribable. My bed became a focal point of my agitation. It took on a personality of its own. Sometimes it insisted, *Get out, get out!* Other times it appeared to beckon me, cunningly, with a promise that if I crawled back in, I would find peace. When I slept, which was seldom, I had the sensation of falling or suffocating or running in the darkness—just running and running.

The days turned into weeks, the weeks into months. How does one endure the unendurable? Only God knows! Every night I prayed I would not awaken in the morning; I pleaded with God to take me home to be with Him. There were precious few times when I felt a tiny bit of normalcy creep back into my life. And even those momentary reprieves would be replaced with bizarre feelings of agitation and anxiety mixed with debilitating depression.

Before this nightmare began, if I didn't get enough sleep at night, I could take a short nap during the day. Invariably, the nap would revive me. These naps that I occasionally enjoyed in the past now took on a horror of their own. I would begin to fall asleep only to be jolted wide awake by a jerking sensation that sent chills of fear down my spine. I felt terrorized by shadows of blackness ready to pounce—ever eager to bring more anguish and pain into my fragile, disjointed mind, and body.

A poem by Emily Dickinson reflected my misery.

I felt a cleaving in my mind
As if my brain had split;
I tried to match it, seam by seam,
But could not make them fit.

The thought behind I strove to join
Unto the thought before,
But sequence ravelled out of reach
Like balls upon the floor.

Farewell, Little Red Hen

My carefully made plans could not work. Little Red Hen would have to go it alone. I would no longer be her soul-mate. I could remember none of my goals; I was incapable of formulating new ones. It would be some time before I could understand that it is better for others to have their own plans and that God's plan is best of all. For now, I could only fling myself onto God's mercy and into the care of my physicians.

Chapter Two: Little Red Hen

CHAPTER THREE
Mock Oranges

James 1:6-8 *How tragic for those tortured and duplicitous souls who are tossed about like angry seas and howling winds. Surely, they will not receive God's blessings.*

Chapter Three: Mock Oranges

The contrast of the vibrant orange against the deep green of the foliage was exquisite. I wanted to snatch an orange directly off a tree and eat it. It was the fall Jim and I moved to Tucson, and I was enthralled by the most spectacular trees laden with luscious-looking fruit. "You're welcome to pick some, but beware!" cautioned the friends we were visiting for Thanksgiving.

Much to my disappointment, these oranges weren't sweet, edible ones, but instead, sour. They had limited practical use, maybe for marmalade. They did look marvelous, but inside they were dramatically different from their outward appearance. Technically, these trees are called sour orange. Our friends described them as surprise, mock oranges.

I, too, was only a mockery of what I looked to be. I had no idea, though, how **much** different I was on the inside than I appeared on the outside. Then I met Dr. Carl Hammerschlag. Before meeting this remarkable man, I was unaware I had stuffed, had covered over, a multitude of emotions. I'd become so proficient at burying my feelings with activity that I could no longer recognize what constituted my natural, legitimate reactions. This accumulation of "black stuff" I'd been storing was churning and burning and, like the proverbial volcano, would spew forth one day. The eruption came with the overdose of estrogen.

Dulling the Pain

Even the overdose didn't get me completely down, at least initially. When I was feeling dreadful that fall, I determined to "pull myself up by my bootstraps" and find a project. And that's what I did! I planned a surprise 50th birthday party for Jim. There were 125 guests; it was loads of work, and the misery didn't cease. I've since discovered that many times frenzied activity is the anesthetic that dulls the pain of a wounded spirit. When I threw myself full force into the birthday project, I had hoped to forget the anguish of brokenness, of discouragement, of not being perfect.

> **Frantically busy people assure themselves that they're needed; they're useful; they're indispensable. Their world depends on them. Things are happening in their lives. They're breathless when they answer the phone: "Oh, will I ever get everything done? . . . You have no idea what it's like to be as busy as I am!"**
>
> **These very ones volunteer to do things because no one else will. They collect for fund-raising drives**

around the neighborhood because they are certain they, or someone dear to them, will get the designated, dreaded disease if they don't do their part—more than their part. Their energy is depleted; they have nothing left to invest in the joys closest to their hearts.

Of course, some individuals are taxed with legitimate burdens almost too much to bear. Others, though, create a whirlwind of needless activity in an ill-disguised attempt to block all varieties of personal pain.

An Initial Therapy Session

I went to my first meeting with Dr. Hammerschlag with fear and trepidation. I'd heard plenty of uncomplimentary things about psychiatrists. I'd already conferred with many doctors, and the idea of seeing "a shrink" was disconcerting, and frankly, somewhat embarrassing.

If you recognize that you need to consult with a psychiatrist, and you can find the financial resources to do so, you may still be apprehensive about what might be involved. Tracing my initial visit with Dr. Hammerschlag may be helpful to you.

So tall that he blocked the light streaming in from the open door, Dr. Carl Hammerschlag came directly over to me. Introducing himself, he offered, "May I get you something to drink—some tea perhaps?" Dr. Hammerschlag's resonating, deep voice intrigued me, sounding much like I'd imagined God's voice. He asked me where I'd like to sit. I chose, then sat. He sat down opposite me and, methodically, began taking off his shoes. Then he lit a candle on the table between us. Unfurling his long limbs, he leaned back in his chair and directed, "Tell me why you've come to see me."

I stammered, stuttered, and stopped periodically to catch my breath. Not willing to spare a single detail, I gave him the entire run-down on how I'd been victimized by the toxic dose of estrogen and how my life was out of control because of this horrendous thing that had happened to me.

He listened thoughtfully, and when I'd finally run out of steam he said, "Perhaps we can work together. You need to know this 'experience' will likely be the most difficult task you've ever undertaken. Are you willing to work? Are you willing to see some things in a whole new way? Are you willing to make some changes in your life? Many people, maybe most, aren't. If you'll commit to this work, I'll walk this journey with you."

An agreement was reached between us that day—an agreement that would alter my life.

Choosing a Therapist

I should imagine that most people want to trust a chosen therapist right from the start. Should you have any reservations about the individual you see, find someone else.

In your vulnerable state, you must feel comfortable enough to confide in your therapist; you must be in a safe place. You're unique and precious, and finding one who treats you with dignity is critical to the healing process.

Confused Parental Roles

Dr. Hammerschlag and I began our journey together talking about my growing up years. I'd lived for 18 years in a home where the parental roles were confused and unsettling. Even though Dad was not unkind to me, he was emotionally unable to model fatherhood. He had been ridiculed by an older brother, embarrassed by teachers, made to feel "less-than." These episodes contributed to his being tentative and insecure about many things. Mother made phone calls for him, took care of the finances, made all the plans and arrangements. My dad was a hard worker, but he was not the emotional or spiritual leader of our family.

I've learned that all young girls need to have a male role model to love them, cherish them, and to help point the way toward healthy relationships with men. Uncle Sonny, who lived in the same yard as we, helped me to feel valued and protected. I spent nearly as much time with Uncle Sonny as I did with my dad.

Not THAT Job!

The summer I turned 16, Mother insisted I get a job. The only position I could find was working in a canning factory a few miles from our farm. The shift was from 4:00 PM until 11:00 PM. This meant I would have to drive through an unsafe area at night. Uncle Sonny was shoveling weeds in the yard when I came home from the interview. He could tell I was upset and asked why.

Tearfully, I stammered, "I'm afraid of driving home from the factory late at night. But Mom says I have to take this job."

"The h--l you do! No niece of mine is going to work at that factory. It's just not safe." Quickly, he grabbed me by the hand, and off we marched to our house. Uncle Sonny flung open the front door and hollered, "Lucile, get out here!" When she dutifully came, he told her what he thought of her and her idea. And that was the end of that. Uncle Sonny seemed to be the only one to get Mom's attention. With Mother, I never knew when the other shoe was going to drop.

Meeting Jim's Parents

Before long it was the early 60's. All my plans were falling into place. I was in college studying to be a teacher, and I'd met a wonderful, highly motivated young man who cherished me and wanted me to share my life with him. Life was good and going "according to Connie."

"It went well, didn't you think?" I had gone to meet Jim's parents. Because Jim and I had talked of marriage, I felt this first encounter to be of utmost importance. I was certain Jim's mom and dad would approve of me. After all, I was conscientious, wholesome, and at least reasonably successful—this girl they were about to meet.

Jim's mother greeted me with a sweet hug. I was immediately drawn to her. I perceived Jim's father to be reserved, maybe a little aloof, but he was cordial. We had a good time that weekend, and I had a sense of well-being as we drove back to our homes.

Well-Being Shattered

I was ill-prepared for the letter Jim received from his father the following week. It read something like this: "Don't bring 'that girl' back here, ever again! As a matter of fact, don't bring any girls here unless it's your grandmother or your Aunt Robbie."

My heavens! What had precipitated that outburst? Obviously, what Jim's dad was feeling on the inside didn't match what he had demonstrated to me on the outside.

I was crestfallen, devastated. Jim was, too. What had gone wrong? What was bad about **me**? Once again, those terrible feelings of worthlessness surfaced and filled my heart with dread and discouragement. I cried and cried.

But the letter didn't change our plans to marry. Just once more before the wedding, I saw Jim's parents. Jim's Aunt Robbie invited me to join the family for Christmas dinner. Jim and I were there when his parents arrived. His father, Ralph, marched over to him and said, "Get your coat!" and off Jim and his parents went, leaving me alone in a houseful of people who were virtual strangers. They were gone for a couple of hours; it seemed an eternity. When they returned, Jim looked ashen and shaken. We left immediately. On the way back to my place I learned what had happened. Jim's parents told him he would be ruining his life if he married me.

Their dream for him was to graduate from Colorado State University with a degree in vocational agriculture. Then he could come back to their little town and teach school. And now he was about to throw all that away. They had determined: Jim wouldn't finish college; I wouldn't finish college; we wouldn't be able to survive; we'd have a baby right away, a baby we couldn't afford or care for. What dire predictions! Whatever was to become of us?

Yes, We Would Marry!

Undaunted, we set our wedding date for February 9,

my brother's birthday. "If you go ahead with the wedding, I will not come!" Ralph admonished. Eventually, he said he might consider attending but only if there were no more than 50 guests present. How he'd determined this arbitrary number, we had no idea.

As the wedding date grew closer, the subject of the rehearsal dinner arose. Under no circumstances was he, Ralph, going to pay for a rehearsal dinner, so Jim and I decided to have only birthday cake, celebrating my brother's birthday, with punch and coffee after the rehearsal.

Ralph did come to the wedding after all—even though we had more than 50 guests. The ceremony and weekend honeymoon in the beautiful Rocky Mountains went smoothly.

Ultimately, I graduated from college and taught kindergarten and first grade for many years. Jim went on to law school. He is now in a large law firm. Our first child was born five years after we were married, and we were able to provide for both Andy and his brother, Jay. All of Ralph Teilborg's pessimistic prognostications came to naught.

I wish I could tell you that all was well after that initial confrontation with Ralph about the wedding. I wish I could tell you that once Dad Teilborg observed that I was a loving, conscientious wife and good mother, he changed his ideas about me. But alas, that was not to be. He has hurt my heart over and over again throughout the years of our marriage. The harder I have tried to please him, the more contentious he's become.

Search for the Right Gift

Ralph seldom acknowledged the gifts I so carefully chose for him. More often than not, I had selected something he deemed unsatisfactory.

Then one day I exclaimed to Jim, "I've finally found it—the perfect gift for your dad!" I discovered one could order seasonal fruit to be sent as a gift every month of the year. I knew that Ralph enjoyed fresh fruit.

"I don't know?" was Jim's dubious reply. "That's a little out of our price range." But there was no stopping me. You would have thought I'd found the Holy Grail!

"We'll make it a birthday and Father's Day gift. Oh, he'll really be pleased!" So we ordered the fruit.

I waited anxiously for Ralph to acknowledge receipt of his first shipment of fruit. No response. Months went by with no comment from Jim's dad. But one Sunday during a family gathering at a restaurant, he startled me. Rarely did he acknowledge my presence.

"Connie, can I ask you to do a big favor for me?" Were my ears deceiving me? Was Dad Teilborg actually asking me to do something for him?

"Yes, of course, whatever it is, I'd be delighted to do it," I eagerly responded. Was Ralph's heart beginning to soften toward me? I could barely dare believe it, and I was thrilled.

"You know that fruit you've been sending me? Well, I'd like for you to stop doing that immediately. It's not good fruit, and besides, it's a big nuisance getting it in the mail every month."

Our younger son, Jay, was sitting next to me. He heard me gasp. Jay knows my heart. He knew I was devastated. He put his hand on my arm and squeezed it. Hurriedly, I excused myself and left the restaurant. Jay followed. I groped my way to the car, all the while fumbling through my purse for the key. I snatched it from my purse, jammed it into the lock, and ripped the car door open. I crumpled onto the seat sobbing uncontrollably.

"Mom, that mean thing that Grandpa just said to you? Why don't you just stop trying to please him? He never likes what you do for him anyway."

"You're right, Jay," I cried. But still I was not ready to admit defeat, at least not yet.

Not Ready to Give Up

Just as Jay knew my heart, so did Jim's dad. He had an uncanny knack of recognizing just where, when, and how to wound me the most. Sometimes, in the middle of an event I had carefully planned, Ralph would announce he was leaving for home. One Christmas was no exception. Young Jay had just begun to painstakingly read his small part of the Christmas story.

Abruptly, his grandfather jumped out of his chair and instructed Jim's mother to, "Get your coat. We're getting out of here—now!"

Indelibly imprinted on my brain is the look on little Jay's face. He sat stoically for a moment or two. Then, carefully, he closed his book and began to cry softly.

Hurt—But Not Right?

Bill Thrall, the founding elder of our church, Open Door Fellowship, cautions, "Just because you're hurt doesn't mean you're right." My flawed part? I was wrong not to confront Ralph with his outrageous behavior early on in our relationship. Like the mock orange, I appeared to him completely different on the outside than I was feeling on the inside. I'd allowed him to bruise, batter, and bludgeon me with his words and actions. I was determined to suffer in silence; I thought it the noble thing to do. I'd pretend all was well, nothing amiss, that we were just one happy family.

I tenaciously believed there was a magic set of keys in my pocket. All the right keys were there. The only problem? I hadn't yet found the one—that special one—that would unlock Ralph's heart. But sooner or later I would. I was convinced of that!

Jim, also, was unable to challenge his father. He was the apple of his dad's eye. He'd already disappointed his father once, by marrying me. He didn't want to topple further off the pedestal his father had created for him. If Jim, or I, had summoned the courage early on in our marriage to confront Ralph with his destructive behavior, I might have a relationship with him today.

I remember one of the most freeing days of my life. Jim's dad had chided me for inviting his and Mom Teilborg's relatives to our home for Thanksgiving dinner. "That was a particularly foolish idea," he curtly announced.

At long last, I sadly responded, "You know, Dad Teilborg, it seems as if you truly do hate me."

"Well no, I don't hate you. I just don't like you," he brusquely retorted.

Hey, Don't Worry!

I felt like doing handstands, somersaults, twirling around and around in circles saying, *Yes, yes, yes!* In my heart I had known all along that Dad Teilborg didn't like me. In the past when I'd mention the possibility to Jim, his standard response was, "Oh, I'm sure he likes you fine. That's just the way he is. Don't worry about it."

If you've been on the receiving end of that kind of advice, you know that's not much help. When someone tells you not to worry about something you're already concerned about, the problem is exaggerated. It makes you feel guilty about your

concern. Then you worry about worrying. Soon you're doubting the validity of your emotions. Your self-esteem plummets. You're set up to be further victimized.

I know things about Ralph today that I didn't know back then. Ralph's mother had taken his identical twin brother, Richard, to town to live with her after a divorce that was considered particularly taboo in those days. She left Ralph on the farm to live with his dad. Most assuredly, Dad Teilborg felt abandoned by his own mother and undoubtedly grew up not trusting women. And especially, he was not about to trust me, the one who had taken his precious first-born from him.

Ralph had few tools to deal with his emotions. He had no place to turn for help. The way he protected himself was to build impenetrable walls. In my situation, the more eager I was to please Jim's dad and to do whatever I could to win his favor, the further he withdrew. The harder I tried, the higher the walls he constructed to keep me out.

Who's In Control?

The one who cares the least in a relationship is often the one who is in control. The other principal in this specific type of dysfunctional relationship is incredulous about the insensitivity, the sarcasm, the scorn. "How can such things be happening? . . .

and over an extended period? If only I keep trying, I'll see improvement . . . won't I? If I just play the mock orange role a bit longer, then he'll be kinder . . . won't he?"

Even when the aggrieved party tries shutting out the bitter words, the non-verbal signals say it all. The venomous looks, the sardonic sneers, the flailing of arms, the abrupt stomping from a room, cut new, and progressively deeper, wounds in the heart of the other.

In May of 1990, Ralph learned our son Andy was to be married. In a phone conversation Dad Teilborg pronounced, "Now you're going to get to see what it's like to have to contend with a daughter-in-law!" Then he hung up. To him I was, and had always been, "a thing" with which to contend. His disapproval continued to define our relationship.

Sometime later, I drove to Sun City to pick up Jim's mother for our Tuesday outing, a regular event we both enjoyed. Normally I tried to avoid Ralph and not allow him to hurt my heart. But that day when I arrived, he cornered me while Jim's mom was in the bathroom. It was his chance to share with me some "uncomplimentary things" his relatives had, supposedly, said about me.

At long last, I finally got it! When I told the story to Dr. Hammerschlag, he responded, "Enough already,

Connie! The old man detests you. Give him the space he wants from you. You're as tenacious as a pit bull! You've tried for thirty years; now give it a rest. It really has little to do with you," C.H. encouraged me to see. "It wouldn't have mattered. No one would have been good enough for Ralph's Golden Boy!"

I didn't have the magic key after all. The lock to Ralph's heart is on the inside; he's chosen not to open the door to me. Ralph loves his son, Jim. He likes his grandsons, Andy and Jay. He's fond of his great-granddaughters, Allie and Mia. He doesn't want me to be part of his life. And that's my reality!

Why have I spent so much time in my life preoccupied with Jim's father? Maybe it's just my stubbornness and pride, but when Jim's parents moved to Arizona, I believed my heart's desire for a healthy family would be answered in them. His mom would be a surrogate mother to me. I hoped and prayed his dad would see the light and want to be like a father to me. My dream was in vain. Ralph Teilborg is not my dad and he doesn't want to be! I am not his daughter. Ralph still wants his son back.

Finding the Truth

> **Do you think you've been a mock orange for someone? In your distorted view of reality, you've thought that by smothering your feelings, by denying your needs, you could eventually gain the acceptance, respect, the love of another. You're seeing that none of these things can be bought.**

You must *never* give up your right to be treated with kindness and dignity! For years and years I pretended that "sticks and stones could break my bones, but words would never harm me." They could, would, and did!

It may take awhile for you to believe—and then integrate into your being—the concept that another person's outrageous behavior may have little to do with you. You did not precipitate that person's actions and reactions. You don't have to continue masquerading as a mock orange. You can delight in your rainbow journey allowing God to exhibit to you the beauty of the orange band. You can witness the blending of the red with the orange—and, more happily, move on.

As I was learning how badly I had missed the rainbow, I could see I had mountains of unhealthy thinking to overcome. Yes, yes indeed, it was proving to be very difficult work. Dr. Hammerschlag was right; it was the hardest task I'd ever attempted. I had thought I could figure out the truth, manage it, manipulate it.

"So, what is the truth?" C.H. asks. "The truth is always closer to what we feel in our hearts than what we know in our heads. The body knows more than the mind chooses to acknowledge." If I continued to ignore what I felt, it would eventually kill me.

It nearly did!

CHAPTER FOUR
Yellow Ducks in a Row

Ecclesiastes 3:1 *Believe there is a right time for all things: God's time.*

What would our lives be like without sunny yellow? This third band of the rainbow represents bright optimism, does it not? . . . Unfortunately, not always. Sometimes yellow's perky boldness manifests itself as a blustery, unwarranted assurance. Even worse, this breezy misplaced self-confidence can presage a dark, dark time ahead.

The Joke's on Whom?

It was just another fashion show at our church's annual women's retreat, or so we assumed. "Presenting 'Women of Open Door,'" the emcee announced. "You'd recognize them anywhere." Ah, I thought. This should be fun: a satire on some of my friends!

But as the first lady pranced down the runway, I was puzzled that she wasn't outlandishly attired. In fact, her outfit was lovely. As Sandy drew closer, I remarked to those around me, "Gracious! That skirt and jacket look just like mine. What? They are mine!" I was so surprised that I heard little of the moderator's comments describing the outfit and me. When Sandy got on stage, she slowly and deliberately opened up the accordion-folded booklet she'd been carrying. It showed a mother duck and her little, yellow ducklings in a perfect row behind her. The women were delighted with the parody of me. We all had a good laugh.

Sandy had asked Jim to sneak one of my finest outfits—one that I wouldn't miss for a few days. She'd stopped by his office to pick it up. I was completely fooled.

Not Really a Laughing Matter

It's amusing to make light of those of us who like to have their ducks in a row. But sometimes sarcastic remarks made tongue-in-cheek, "Of course, Connie wouldn't have anything out of place in her home," or "I don't have my whole month planned like Connie," can be ill-disguised attempts at covering up insecurity or jealousy.

Those who mock our attempts to control our lives don't understand how rigorously we must work to keep the ducks perfectly aligned. And often, it's not only our own ducks that have to be monitored, but those of others as well.

Immoderate Responses

Ecclesiastes in the Bible cautions that there is an appropriate time for everything. Sometimes it's a good thing to have your ducks in a row. Sometimes not. The wise teaching in Ecclesiastes cries out for moderation. For nearly fifty years, I couldn't even entertain the idea of moderation. Not only did I want my yellow ducks in a row, I wanted my children's ducks to line up as well.

As they were growing up, the boys had regular chores to do. On Saturdays, they were to clean their rooms. Jay had been dragging his feet this particular day. He'd get easily sidetracked. The phone rang. It was Jay's friend Rodney.

"Can Jay come over to my house to play?"

"Is your room straightened up, Jay? Rodney wants to know if you can play."

"Yep, Mom, it is," he assured me. And out the front door he went.

I was in the middle of a project of my own and didn't have an opportunity to check Jay's room until later that morning. One of his duties had been to clean out his dresser drawers. I opened them. They hadn't been touched. I was livid! It was then that I did the unthinkable. I took every one—yes—every one of the drawers out of his desk and dresser and dumped them **all** in the middle of his bedroom floor. It looked as if a tornado had struck his room. Then I called Rodney's house and told his mother to send Jay home immediately.

As I impatiently waited for Jay, I was filling up with that sort of wickedness we all have somewhere deep inside of us. When Jay arrived, with fiendish delight I carefully took him by the hand and slowly led him to his bedroom. The moment I saw his face, I knew the sinister deed I had done. I had passed on to my son what had been meted out to me as a little girl. It's called evil!

I knelt beside him and put my arms around him. I was crying. He was crying. I told him how sorry I was. And, together, we put the things back into the drawers. It didn't take long. I doubt that either of us will forget that day. And, I hope I will never forget that I am always, within a gnat's breath, of projecting onto others that which was done to me.

My immoderate reaction to Jay's messy room might remind you of times you've treated a child unfairly. The resentments from your past still plague you.

Your child—any child—is a readily accessible victim on whom you're unleashing anger that has little to do with his childish behavior. But making the connection with your own bad experiences can help remind you of healing that must be accomplished in your life to halt the cycle.

Your Car, But . . .

Jim and I had definite ducks-in-a-row guidelines for Andy when we helped him purchase his used, bright yellow Camaro. He was delighted he could drive himself to school; no more embarrassment about Mom taking him. The rules were explicit—directly to and directly from school. And absolutely, positively, no driving around during lunch hour.

It was a lovely fall day and I was on my way to meet a friend for lunch. En route to the restaurant, I took a street not too far from where Andy attended high school. I really had no intention of spying on Andy to see if he had his ducks in a row that day. While waiting at the stop sign, I observed a yellow car barreling through the green light at the intersection. "Wow, that car's moving at a healthy rate of speed," I said to myself. "Well, who can believe this?" It was none other than Andy Teilborg in his banana-yellow car. I was astounded! It was violation enough for him to be driving his car off campus during lunch hour. However, to add insult to injury, with him were about seven other teenagers. The windows were rolled down, his stereo was blasting as I witnessed a profusion of arms and legs draped out of the windows like flags on a ship, wafting in the breeze. I was more than eager to hear Andy's explanation when he got home from school.

"Hi, Honey, how was school?"

"It was O.K."

"Anything exciting happen?"

"Nope."

"What did you have for lunch?" I quizzed. Andy looked at me suspiciously.

"I don't remember. Oh, yeah, we had Mexican food."

"Was it good?"

"Umm, it was all right, I guess."

"Andy, if I told you I was at the intersection of 7th Street and Dunlap at 12:15 today, what would you think?" His face turned white, then a bright red as he sheepishly replied,

"Well, I'd think I'd have some explaining to do." Andy's banana-yellow boat was docked for a few days . . . and with few exceptions, Andy lined his yellow ducks up fairly well after that.

Someone New to Supervise

No one close to me was exempt from my persistent inclination to direct. Although I had yet to meet Amy, I was more than ready to help her line up her ducks.

Andy played football while attending the University of Arizona. He called us one week to tell us we would be sitting at the game with his new friend, Amy, a lovely, tall blonde. Their friendship developed into love. After Amy received her degree in sociology from the U of A, she wasn't certain what she wanted to do and was exploring her options. She needed a place to stay. We offered to have her live with us.

Not having a daughter, I believed this to be my golden opportunity to be mother to a girl. I jumped right in, mouth first, and began to help Amy plan her life. I thought she would make an excellent teacher, so together we went to explore her options. She enrolled in a fifth-year teacher training program.

I became far too enmeshed in Amy's life. Misunderstandings developed. I knew little in those days of saying it straight out the way it is. I suspected our relationship was not developing in a healthy way; I just didn't know how to line those particular ducks-in-a-nice-tidy-row.

It was during this time, before I had been taught about "recovery," that my friend Ann suggested I attend a 12-step meeting. I will always be grateful for that wise advice. It helped immensely. I had many deeply rooted issues to ferret out; it was a beginning.

Eventually, Amy and Andy married, and I continued to work on my recovery. Just when I thought I'd learned a particular lesson, I was presented with yet another opportunity to practice.

An Escalating Incident

It was silly, really. Isn't that usually how misunderstandings develop? A friend and I decided to start a recycling business for designer clothes. In my zeal to get things moving, I remembered I'd given Amy an expensive, yellow dress when she was living with us. With the gift of the dress, I had elicited from her the assurance she really did want it and would, indeed, wear it.

I called Amy. "If you're wearing the dress I gave you and are enjoying it, fine. If not, would you like to recycle it?"

"I have no idea where that dress is. I think it got lost in one of my moves," Amy replied.

I was stunned! How could a dress worth hundreds of dollars just "get lost" while moving? I didn't say that, however. What I said was, "Oh? O.K." We chatted for a few minutes about other things, then hung up. I was fuming.

After I commiserated for a few minutes with my business partner about the lost yellow dress, she, quite indignantly, demanded that I call Amy back and tell her to locate that dress, post haste. So I made the ill-advised call. Amy was backed into a corner and she came out swinging. We both said things that were hurtful to the other.

Even my giving had conditions attached to it. Now I know that giving needs to be clean—no strings attached. The gift of freedom must accompany the material gift: freedom for the recipient to do with the present what she chooses to; latitude to keep it, treasure it, give it away, or I suppose, trash it!

Paying a Bitter Price

As a result of that encounter, I didn't see Amy, Andy, or my new granddaughter, Allie, for five months. Andy came alongside Amy and supported her stance. It was the right thing for him to do—stand by his wife. It was a painful period. I learned things in that time I couldn't or wouldn't have learned any other way.

Because I didn't hear from Andy throughout the summer and didn't know if or when I would, I wrote him a letter. At the time I considered my letter to be judicious and compassionate. But gradually I became aware that I was still trying to get everyone to shape up to my standards. Today, I would send a revised version of that letter, one that would not be instructive or didactic but, instead, filled with kindness and love.

Gratefully, now Amy and I have a healthier relationship. I don't try to be her mother; she has a mother. I hope I've learned my lesson, and my prayer is that I can, and will, be a loving, supportive, caring, and compassionate mother-in-law.

Anger Makes Us Ugly

My sessions with Dr. Hammerschlag continued to be productive as he helped me deal with these important, interpersonal issues. It was difficult learning to express my feelings about things I'd long since buried. And most of the painful issues in my life had not been brought to proper closure. Dr. Hammerschlag warned me, "Holding on to anger makes us ugly. It fills our souls with distrust that comes out in our relationships and in our work. Anger masks our fear."

The frozen rage, depression (de-pressed; pressed down) deep inside of me had never been brought to the light to be exposed. Only when a level of trust has been developed can a person face the demons within. I didn't know how to trust. This sense of trust is a critical part of the personality development of a child. That development had been short-circuited in my life. I couldn't trust my parents to cherish me. At times I couldn't trust my husband to protect my heart. I couldn't trust my children to understand me. I found it very difficult to trust anyone—even God, most especially God. Although I had a relationship with the Living Lord, I wasn't convinced He always had my best interests at heart. Consequently, I felt I needed to be ever vigilant, ever tenacious, keeping my own ducks-in-my-own-rows.

Darkness Drains the Light

It was summer again, almost a year from the overdose. I had been seeing Dr. Hammerschlag for several months. I knew I was making progress, but often it seemed like three steps forward, two backward. My ducks were swimming helter-skelter and I couldn't round them up, couldn't get them back into rows. I knew I was spiraling downward and I was frightened. I couldn't wait in the rain; couldn't trust God to lead my journey. As the summer progressed, the days grew darker and darker. Memories from the past continued to bubble out of the murky blackness buried within me. It felt, as my friend Carolyn so aptly described, "Like open heart surgery without any anesthetic."

Depression was smothering me; I couldn't get my

breath. My aching head strained in the attempt to stop distorted thoughts. I struggled to stand up straight. My legs and arms dangled, further weighing down my already lead-laden body.

I wore the same two or three outfits. They were clean, I guess, but merely covered my shell. I don't remember putting on makeup. I imagine I didn't. Food tasted like cotton. I smelled nothing. Friends tell me my eyes shrank to tiny slits peering from a chalky, expressionless face. Swirls of cold, gray winds encompassed my body and spirit. I was the walking dead.

I Had to Do Something

When, how, and where the idea first took root in my mind, I don't recall. It was gradual. When I could mutter a few words to a friend, it was about death and dying. Earlier, on one of my best days, I visited with a friend who had tried to take her life when she was in high school. "How did you come to that place? What did you feel? Were you afraid? Do you think God forgives those who kill themselves?"

Judging Harshly

If you haven't been there, please don't judge too harshly those of us who have. I've listened to comments like these and made many of them myself in the past:

"What a selfish act it is to take your own life."

"That's nonsense—pain too hard to bear."

"I guess he didn't care anything about his family or friends or he would not have done that horrible thing."

"I think she was just trying to get even with so-and-so by her suicide."

Ending the Pain

In reality, I wasn't thinking any of those things. I wasn't thinking. My impression: I can't stand this any longer. I must end this pain!

Jim and I were at our cabin for a long September weekend. Stuck in quicksand, I was slowly, diabolically, pulled downward. God doesn't hear my prayers; He doesn't care, I was sure. There is no way out. I will die to end the pain!

Jim left for a few hours to go fishing. While he was gone, I tried to walk in the forest. It was a supreme effort just to put one foot in front of the other. The beauty of the woods I'd so enjoyed in the past frightened me now; the trees took on sinister and terrifying distortions. The blue jays called to me, "Kill yourself! Kill yourself!" Even the dear little chipmunks and squirrels taunted me as they scurried about.

I staggered back to the cabin. I must find Jim's duffle bag. That's how I would end it all; that's what I would use. Ah, there's the gun. Quickly, how to do it. Jim's mother had knitted an afghan for us to use at the cabin; I would take that with me out into the forest to lie on. But do I put the gun in my mouth or to my temple? I had to be careful. What was I forgetting? I didn't want to mess this up.

What was that noise? Sounded like a car coming. Who'd be driving up? I stood, paralyzed with fear—fear that my plan would be thwarted. The sound came closer and closer. Now it was turning onto our road. Oh, no, it couldn't be. **Jim!** What was he doing back so early?

"Hi, honey. The wind blew me off the lake so I decided to call it a day and come back to be with my sweetheart. Con, what's wrong? You look strange; you're so pale." I fell to the floor in a heap, sobbing hysterically.

I didn't let Jim know how close I'd come to taking my life that morning. God, the Author and Creator of the universe, the One who calmed the angry sea, just as effortlessly brought the wind to a mountain lake to spare the life of one of His children. I believe that's what happened that momentous day.

Jim went with me to see Dr. Hammerschlag on Tuesday. In Jim's presence, I painfully told C.H. what I'd almost accomplished. He extracted a promise from me that I would not entertain those thoughts, not ever again! He suggested it might be time for me to be hospitalized.

Something must be done to break the cycle of depression. The shock of what I'd almost done jolted me back to the reality of life and, ultimately, the finality of death.

CHAPTER FIVE
Two-Headed Green Snake

II Timothy 1:7 *A fearful spirit is not the Lord's doing. Instead, He fills us with strength, courage, and love.*

What was I to do? Where was I to go?

Dr. Hammerschlag would not make my decision for me. "Do you want to be hospitalized? Do you want to try a new medication? Can we trust you not to hurt yourself while we give the medicine a chance to work?"

Through my heaving sobs I managed to say, "I **need** a break."

I would be admitted, locally, to Camelback Hospital and stay there for a week or so. Although Dr. H. had not utilized this particular facility for some time, he thought I would receive good care. As Jim led me to the door, I collapsed into Dr. H's arms. I cried the last tears I had left as Jim stood helplessly by.

"This has got to be right," I begged to thin air as Jim and I drove the short distance to the care center. We followed the signs pointed toward admission. It all seemed make-believe; I felt suspended in time and space.

My mind was whirling with distorted thoughts. Must I put on the application for my driver's license renewal that I'd been in a mental hospital? What if I decide to teach again? Would they allow me to be responsible for young children knowing I'd been hospitalized for clinical depression? Maybe I don't get to vote if I've been in treatment! What if?...What if?...What if?...

As we were being escorted to my room, I glanced at a large sign on the wall. The posted group meeting times didn't include me anywhere:

GROUP MEETING TIMES

ALCOHOLICS	9:00 AM
HEROIN ADDICTS	10:00 AM
COCAINE ADDICTS	11:00 PM
SEX ADDICTS	1:00 PM
ANOREXICS	2:00 PM
BULIMICS	3:00 PM
OCCUPATIONAL THERAPY	4:00 PM

In the midst of my fog of depression, I knew that something was awry. My luggage had to be checked at the nurses' station to make certain it didn't contain anything I could use to hurt myself.

"Hmm, now where will we put you?" mused the orderly charged with my check-in. While he was deciding, a confused young man walked agitatedly by me.

"O.K. gang, tonight's the night I'm reading my chart."

"No, not tonight, Eric," responded one of the nurses.

"Yes, yes tonight. Tonight it's gonna be. I've been planning this all day, and I won't be put off; nope, not one more day. You guys have to let me read my chart. I know you do 'cause it's the law!" By this time, my head was throbbing.

"How can I get well in this place?" I anguished to Jim. When a pathetic, disoriented bag of bones sucking on a cigarette was introduced as my roommate, my apprehension skyrocketed. I knew I must flee!

Jim asked for a release form, but we were told we'd have to wait for Dr. Hammerschlag to sanction my departure. He was observing a Jewish holy day and unavailable. Finally, after what seemed an eternity, Jim got me released to his care.

"I'm really not as sick as those people in that hospital," I assured Jim on the ride home. "I'll take the new medication. I know it will work. It **has** to work!"

I suppose I was on some sort of adrenaline high. I thought I'd had a reprieve from the blackness . . . it was short lived.

Blackness Here to Stay?

There was never to be a pot of gold for me. . . . Nor could I ever see a rainbow . . . no beautiful blending of red with orange into yellow and then merging with green. . . . Only fearsome distortions bled throughout my consciousness.

The little wooden box sat undisturbed on the coffee

table throughout all my sessions with Dr. Hammerschlag. I'd wondered about it but hadn't asked. One day I was bemoaning my reality—I couldn't recall when I hadn't been depressed. "I guess I've always been like this and always will be," I despondently sighed.

"You've forgotten, Connie, that you've had times of laughter, even times of joy since the overdose. See if you can reflect on those times."

"I'm frightened the blackness will never, ever go away."

C.H. reached over and picked up the wooden box. "The Indians tell a story with this box." As he lifted the top a bit, the head of a green snake came out one side. When Dr. H. lifted the top further, another snake's green head shot out from the other side. "Indian lore teaches us if you're frightened and try to run away from your fears, the snakes will chase you. First one scoots out, sticks his head in your path and you're terrified. You run even faster to veer away from him. When you do that, the snake's other green head comes from the opposite direction to strike at you."

Stand Still and Wait

"Let's think about this for a moment," Dr. Hammerschlag encouraged. "When you are fearful, instead of trying to outrun the green-headed snakes, what if you just stand motionless and wait? What happens then? Well, both heads of the snake come out. One green head sees the other. They are terrified of the sight of themselves. They retreat into their box and you are safe."

What had I learned about fear? I'd learned that I can't outrun my fears. I'd learned I must be willing to acknowledge them no matter how deeply imbedded they are. I must pull my fears out from the darkness of the cellars of my life—the places where I'd been belittled, even terrorized. But how long was this process going to take? I didn't believe I could hang on much longer.

A Change of Scene

Jim thought the change of scenery would do me good. The flight to Durango was smooth. Trees were beginning to adorn themselves in autumn colors. I took little pleasure in any of it. The new medication, Zoloft, was not working. It was making me jittery, just as Prozac had.

The high I'd experienced after leaving Camelback Hospital earlier on had vanished. We spent the weekend in the Colorado mountains in somber anticipation of what lay ahead.

On the way back to Phoenix, I hoped and prayed our plane would crash. "What about Jim?" you ask. I wasn't concerned about Jim; I didn't even think of him. My terror was that I, involuntarily, continued to breathe life into my body. Why couldn't I just stop breathing? It would be so simple then. And the pain would be gone.

My Last Hope

But we got home safely. Sleep didn't come that night. Finally, I groped for the tape I had ordered months ago from Alpha Care. With hands trembling, I thrust the tape into the VCR. It took several attempts at viewing before the peacefulness of the facility penetrated my consciousness.

This is my last hope, I told myself as the sun came peeking over the horizon.

I made my desperate call to Alpha Care at 7:00 AM. By 10:00 that same morning, Jim and I were on the plane heading to San Diego. I wept exhausted, bitter tears for most of the trip. We rented a car and wound our way up the coast of California.

The house was serene, the grounds green and lush, and the flowers soft and delicate. Dare I hope I could heal here? How my body, mind, and spirit longed for rest!

We were ushered into Joni's office. Somehow Jim and I filled out the necessary paper work. We were left alone to say good-by. I clung to Jim and moaned softly. Reluctantly, he left me a few moments later.

Trying to Try

Shelly appeared immediately. She'd take me to the

clinic to have a physical, she announced. During the entire trip in the van, she chatted incessantly. About what, I have no idea. When we returned it was dinnertime. "Tonight's pizza night," I was informed. Shelly introduced the other patients seated at the dining room table. They looked amazingly normal, but there was no way I could talk, let alone eat.

I was assigned to a twin bed situated by itself at one end of a large bedroom. The room was comfortable and tastefully furnished. In my heart I felt a tiny flutter of hope. Shelly went through my things while I listlessly watched her. She took my gold stretch belt—a potential weapon—for lock-up.

The medication I had brought with me was taken, too. Part of me comprehended that the other patients were wandering about—reading, writing in journals, talking, laughing, whatever. I felt separate, detached, probably didn't really belong here.

The evening group session (called Group) was beginning. I was excused so I could get settled in. I unpacked. I guess I must have put my things into the drawers in the dresser and hung my clothes in the closet.

That task done, I sank into a tub full of warm water. What was **that** on the bathtub? My, my. None other than a plastic mother duck and her three yellow ducklings. Automatically, I lined them up in a perfect row behind their mother.

A Safe Place

My roommate, Beverly, was consoling. As I lay in bed waiting for the sleep medication to work, I managed to thank God for Alpha and Dr. Hammerschlag.

I woke up several times that first night, but my terrors seemed to be subsiding a wee bit. Beverly heard me go to the bathroom and asked how I was doing. Her concern touched my heart.

Dr. Henderson, the staff psychiatrist, arrived between 7:15 and 7:30 each morning. He spent extra time with me that first morning. He decided not to prescribe antidepressants until he was certain the Zoloft was out of my system. After his visit, I was called for blood pressure and temperature check. While I was perched on the stool, I noted the little certificate on the wall:

STATE OF CALIFORNIA
ACUTE PSYCHIATRIC CARE FACILITY

Would I fail all over again? I hope not! I pray not! The routine for each day was carefully planned and offered me safety and security:

- **Early Morning Group—12-Step Study—Help Me, God**
- **Individual Sessions**
- **Morning Group Session**
- **Lunch**

- **Individual Sessions**
- **Afternoon Group**
- **Later Afternoon—Aerobics 3x a week—Art Therapy**
- **Dinner**
- **Early Evening—Occupational Therapy—Role Playing—Praise Time**

Dr. Henderson allowed me an early pass to go for a walk with Beverly the second day I was there. The general rule: You weren't to leave the premises until you'd been at Alpha for 72 hours. How odd needing permission to go for a walk. Climbing the steep hill a few blocks from the facility was good exercise and lifted my spirits slightly.

Routine Important

The routine at Alpha was comforting. No surprises! I always knew what was ahead. Wednesdays and Sundays we had outings. Because the average stay at Alpha was four weeks, four different Wednesday activities were arranged:

1. **Outlet store shopping**
2. **Afternoon at the beach**
3. **Miniature golf**
4. **Lunch at a fun restaurant with browsing after**

The first Wednesday was difficult. My fears were unpredictable; they came and went. I was just settling into the routine and had no desire to leave, even for a brief time. We were taken to a quaint restaurant in the Alpha van. I was still shaky from the Zoloft and had little appetite. The other women were all excited about ordering dessert.

"I'm going to have the triple-layer mud pie with loads of whipped cream," gushed Sandra.

Bev exclaimed, "What about the chocolate and caramel cheesecake with the Oreo cookie crust? That sounds divine!"

This banal chatter annoyed me. I just wanted to be left alone; I couldn't care less that we weren't allowed sugar at Alpha. The desserts, as part of the outing, were a treat for the others, however. Later on I would understand.

Our Sunday outing was to attend church, go to lunch, and then to a large drug store to get any sundries we might want. And that's when we'd purchase our contraband. Imagine grown women sneaking around, like super sleuths, to buy chocolate or Werther's Butterscotch Candy.

Relaxing a Bit

As each day passed, I felt less in danger. As I was settling in, my body was settling down. Several therapists were available for us. Tough and bright, Kendall (the only female) made us work exceedingly hard. Mark had the most empathy. He had a unique way of cutting to the chase in a kind, gentle way. Kevin, the case worker, handled the joint session (called conjoint) with our psychiatrists/counselors back home and also with family members. He was responsible for our aftercare planning. On weekends we had two visiting counselors.

Kelly's Problems

As the hours passed, my mind had become less clouded with dark thoughts and I'd begun to notice things and people around me. Kelly, who remains a special friend, drove me bonkers with her constant complaining. "Why can't we watch TV? Why can't we eat sugar or chocolate or whatever?" She railed at anything and everything. On my second Wednesday outing, Kelly sat alone on a bench in the middle of the mall, fuming. She was convinced Alpha was not helping her and was a waste of time, energy, and money.

The next morning in Group, Kelly announced she was leaving. *Good!* I thought to myself. *She's so miserable here and a constant disruption.* I tried to pray for her. After the morning session, she went out to the guest house to journal. The Lord spoke to Kelly's heart and changed it that morning. She decided to stick it out. At afternoon Group she declared she was staying. She was going to begin working with the program instead of against it. The change in her was dramatic; even her countenance changed.

Letting Hate Spew Out

Sometime during my first week, I don't recall which day, the Group time focused on me. The session evolved as I revealed an early childhood memory. Before I knew what was happening, the staff had drawn the blinds to darken the room. One of the team members led me to the middle of the circle. "Tell us how it **felt** to be dragged to the cellar for your beatings. How did you **feel** about the spiders?" I started shaking, broke out in cold sweat, and screamed, "NO, NO, NO!" over and over again. I was huddled over in a ball with my arms wrapped tightly around me. Kendall was in my face yelling, "Tell your mother how you **feel**; tell her. Tell God how you **feel** about His not stopping the beatings." I was screaming at the top of my lungs. One of the staff handed me a foam bat so I could pound on the wall. Later, I was told I shrieked my hatred to my mother. I screamed at God and told Him I hated Him, hated Him for letting me suffer so as a little girl and for permitting me to be in such anguish now.

How could I lose control and act so unladylike? What I do know is that, afterwards, I was emotionally and physically exhausted and exceedingly hoarse. I was given the foam bat to carry with me wherever I'd go for the next 24 hours. I felt lighter though, perhaps even freer. I took a long, peaceful nap that afternoon.

Soon I discovered I could sit for long periods on my bed. Sometimes I'd journal, sometimes just be. I took an occasional nap. Often, I'd just relax in the sun that streamed into the bedroom in the afternoons. I'd sit and think—think about all the years I'd been in such bondage, so locked up inside: fearful, rigid, trapped in my feelings of unworthiness.

Could it be that the frozen rage that had been exposed in my sessions with C.H. was now, at Alpha, beginning to thaw? Could I allow myself to know and candidly talk about the pain deep inside of me? Could I trust this place and the people here?

Truck Driver Talk

Sometimes during Group or individual sessions we used slang expressions and we didn't get our mouths washed out with soap. One day Mark laughingly remarked, "You come to us as sweet, Christian ladies and we turn you into tough-talking truck drivers."

> **It was imperative that we give vent to our feelings even if the initial purging was somewhat unorthodox. Many of us had spent our lives as victims of excessive legalism and extreme rigidity. We'd never learned how to speak candidly without fear of reprisal.**

The crux of the issue is that often legitimate feelings go unexpressed or are suppressed, and these time bombs are potentially far more dangerous than an occasional expletive uttered in frustration or anger. After we'd had plenty of practice getting it out, we would learn how to say it more appropriately.

Where's My Quilt?

Shortly after Beverly left, my new roommate, Jeanine, checked in. She was a beautiful girl and announced to me, almost immediately, that she was a sex addict. "Oh fine, that's just great," I groaned to Kelly.

Kelly and I'd been in the guest house chatting. I returned to my room to discover Jeanine had taken the pretty quilt I'd been given for my bed when Suzanne, the cook/housekeeper, noticed me shivering one morning. Jeanine had ripped it off and put the quilt on her own bed.

Instantly, I reverted back to the old Connie. I was furious! I thought, *how presumptuous. How dare Jeanine do that. What could she be thinking? Surely she knows that's my quilt; after all, it was on my bed. I know I'm not going to like her. She thinks because she's so beautiful she can have whatever she wants!* Outwardly, I said nothing.

A couple of days passed. One afternoon I was talking with Doris, a member of the staff, and brought up the quilt incident. I thought she'd be all over me like a rash and castigate me for not sticking up for myself. Instead, she was contemplative and said, "You need to understand, Connie, that many outwardly beautiful people are used to getting what they want when they want it. Many times it's a curse, rather than a blessing, to be born with such outward perfection. Let's think, together, how you might handle the situation with Jeanine."

Later that afternoon, with my knees knocking, I explained to Jeanine that Suzanne had given me the quilt. I told her that saying things straight out was difficult for me and was one of the reasons I needed to be at Alpha.

"Oh, sorry," she retorted. "I saw it on your bed and thought it was pretty, so I took it." Jeanine gave me back the quilt. Just like that. My, that wasn't so difficult after all!

That same night I awakened to go to the bathroom. Jeanine was awake. She asked if I was having trouble sleeping. "No, I just had to go to the bathroom."

"Would you like me to come over and rub your back?" she inquired. *Oh, no*, I thought. *She's a sex addict and she wants to know if she can rub my back. She likes men, though, not women. Oh dear, what shall I say?*

"I guess that will be all right. Only for a couple of minutes, though, and just stay on top of the covers."

I told Dr. Henderson the next morning. He just smiled and said, "Good for you, Connie. I'm pleased you said what you felt. I've been thinking about you and praying for you. I talked with Dr. Hammerschlag yesterday. He's a fine man and has been concerned about you." Continuing our discussion, Dr. Henderson explained, " I have some good news/bad news for you. The good news: It's not your fault when the depression comes. The bad news: Depression will come but you are learning to develop tools to combat it."

No Thanksgiving Cards

A wave of panic washed over me one unsettling night during my second week at Alpha. I was ambivalently watching a silly movie when, suddenly, a Thanksgiving celebration filled the screen. Instantaneously, I was struck with this thought: What about my Thanksgiving cards (we send cards out at Thanksgiving rather than Christmas)? It was nearly the end of October and we hadn't even taken the family picture. I hadn't written the annual letter. I became so agitated I announced to all that I had to leave. I slept fitfully that night.

Predictably, Fern, the evening nurse, told Mark what had happened. The next morning during Group Mark confronted me. "Did it occur to you, Connie, that you could skip Thanksgiving cards this year? Or, perhaps, you could send out Christmas cards like most of the rest of us do." It hadn't occurred to me, and anyway everybody would be expecting them. Maybe people would think Jim and I were getting a divorce or that some other terrible thing had happened in our family. My mind was racing with these pessimistic possibilities.

My individual session was with Mark that day. We spent the time on my lifelong fear of what others might think of me. It was an exceedingly productive time.

Insurance Problems

It was shortly after the Thanksgiving card episode that my recovery progress was dramatically tested. My insurance company had tentatively approved a week's stay but now required more information. Someone from Arizona was flying in to check on the facility and to interview me. The whole idea was frightening. Monica, the head nurse, said she'd be with me throughout the interview—not to worry.

As scheduled, Fred from the insurance company showed up the next day. I took an immediate dislike to him; he appeared slick and sinister. Fred, Monica, and I were closeted in the back room, Fred starting out with fairly routine questions. Soon the questions became more and more intense and involved very sensitive issues. I became increasingly agitated. On and on he went like a marathon runner. I was soaking up wads of Kleenex with my sobbing. Monica had her arm around me and was glaring at Fred. It didn't deter him; he continued for well over an hour. At one point I told him I had a terrible headache; I was nearly hysterical. "That's too bad," he replied nonchalantly. "This is what I do for headaches." Then he proceeded to show us how he rubbed the back of his head to relieve the pressure.

When, finally, he was finished, I ran out of the room and collapsed in a heap in front of the nurses' station. Someone led me to bed and gave me a tranquilizer. I was lying on my bed, quietly sobbing, when Dr. Henderson walked into our bedroom with **FRED** trailing behind. What's happening? What are they doing here? Why is Dr. Henderson bringing that man in here, into my bedroom?

"Connie, we understand you're upset and we came, together, to tell you that Fred meant you no harm." Now it was Fred's turn.

"I'm truly sorry if I upset you. I had to ask all those questions to determine how long you needed to stay." I yearned to yell at both of them, *get out, just get out*! Of course, I didn't. I just continued to cry.

After Fred left, Dr. Henderson and Monica had a conference about what **really** happened during the interview. Dr. Henderson was furious when he heard the rest of the story. He stayed for dinner that night. He sat at the end of the table and all through dinner talked rapidly, and with animation, into his dictaphone. I'm convinced Fred's insurance company got a letter from

Dr. Henderson with smoke steaming right through the envelope.

Back On Prozac

Each day at Alpha I felt a bit better, a little stronger. Dr. Henderson and Dr. Hammerschlag decided it would be advisable to start me on Prozac once again. They would cut way back on the dosage. It would be given in liquid from a dropper. "How does that sound to you?" they both wanted to know. The first couple of days were fine, but when I woke up the third day, I had a weird sense of foreboding.

Our son Andy had come to visit me. I signed out, and we went for a long walk. After the rigorous exercise, we returned to the guest house to visit. It was a warm day so I attributed the shakiness I was feeling to the heat and the walk up the steep hill. We'd been chatting for a few minutes when Harriet, the staff nurse on duty, came to the door to speak to me. "Gracious!" I said to Andy. "I must have forgotten to sign out." My mind was spinning with anxious thoughts of why Harriet would interrupt me in the middle of Andy's visit. I'd done something wrong; that's always a given. Harriet guided me out the door and into the back courtyard.

"There's something I must tell you." Her eyes filled with tears. "I just discovered that I've been giving you the wrong dosage of Prozac. For the last three days I have given you five times the amount you were to have.

I'm so sorry, so very sorry. Can you ever forgive me?"

I stood in stunned disbelief. Not again! How could this be happening? I reached out and hugged Harriet and assured her that I would forgive her.

During Group, the staff encouraged me to talk about what had transpired. I really didn't have much to say. Another freak accident. I was confused and why did these accidents keep happening to **me**? Mark was concerned that I automatically felt I was the one who had done something wrong when Harriet called me away from my visit to talk with me.

"The bad things that happen around you and to you aren't always your fault, Connie," Mark injected with fervor. "You **must** come to see that." Gradually, I was learning that my self-centered, distorted thinking made me feel solely responsible in circumstances where often I played merely a minor role—if any at all.

Poisoned?

Monday morning when he arrived, Mark announced he would see only two people: Kelly and me. I was surprised since I'd just had "individual" with him on Friday. He called me into the room and closed the door. "I've been troubled about you all weekend, Connie. When I got the word you'd been overdosed, yet once again, I decided we've been missing something. I've been praying and asking God to show me why these accidents continue to happen to you." What Mark said next was shocking! "Do you feel someone tried to poison you? When you were a little girl, did someone try to hurt you by putting something into your mouth? Think back. Think back carefully while I pray for you."

As I lay on the couch listening to Mark pray, I thought, *this is silly. I've just been in the wrong places at the wrong times.* But, as I reflected, I began to feel something stir deep within. My throat started to burn. I felt far, far away. Mark's voice sounded more and more distant. I began crying, softly at first, then more loudly.

Something was happening to me! My mom was putting soap in my mouth! She was washing my mouth out with a wash cloth filled with soap. A corner of the wash cloth slid down my throat. It was gagging me; I was choking! I was trying to push her away but she was stronger. Her fingernails were cutting into my gums. I was going to choke to death. "Make her stop, please make her stop. Won't someone please help me!" I knew where I was. I knew Mark was there. I knew I was screaming, and I was powerless to stop the screams from coming.

Deeply Rooted Fears

What does all of this mean? I'm not certain. Perhaps all along my body had tried to let my mind know that I had deeply rooted fears about being poisoned, about choking to death. I had never acknowledged this fear. It had to be brought forth from the darkness into the light.

And that's what happened that afternoon with Mark. Mother didn't know, or understand, that I truly believed I would die that day she washed my mouth out with soap. Little Connie knew it, but she'd buried it deep in the blackness.

I had a psychological breakthrough that day, I realize. But I believe it was more than that. Through Mark's concerted praying, I feel God was helping me begin to let go of the fears that had bound me these many years: fears of choking; fears of being poisoned; and fears of dying. I was learning—albeit slowly—that only after fear is acknowledged and healed can it be released.

I was gradually appreciating that God is **not** the author of fear, and He is aiding me through my life's journey. If I would trust Him with the colors of my life, He would blend them beautifully in His own time; God would merge them into His flawless, rainbow design for me.

My last night at Alpha, I moved the little, yellow ducklings out of their perfect row.

Chapter Five: Two-Headed Green Snake

CHAPTER SIX
Blue Jay

Isaiah 21:11b-12 *Sentinels know what's going on—day and night.*

The robust blue jay, sitting on an upper branch of a pine tree by our cabin's back porch, let out one of his raucous calls just as I opened the door, "Beware! Beware!" I nearly dropped the peach peelings I was about to throw over the porch to feed the forest animals.

"Now that's a fine good morning, Mr. Blue Jay. You nearly scared me out of my wits! I know it's your job to warn the animals when danger is near. I just wish you could do it a little more softly and gently."

Jays have a reputation; it's well-deserved. They are the tattle-tales, the sentinels of the forest. The ones in our area don't miss a trick. These Steller's Jays are perpetually on guard. Sometimes it's comforting, sometimes not.

Always Alert

Many of us stand guard for ourselves, for others, or a combination of both. I was compelled to be on guard, always, from the time I can remember. I didn't want to do anything to attract attention. Mother, on the other hand, raised a big fuss in front of everyone. She berated grocery clerks, repairmen, and whomever else she judged clumsy or inefficient. Often, when I was with her and she'd start to rant and rave, I'd wish for the floor to cave in so I could fall in with it. I was in a perpetual state of shame at the scenes Mom would make.

In the little, country grade school I attended, I stood out with my white-blonde hair. Many of the children were dark-haired and dark-skinned. During assemblies we were amused by magicians, trick dogs, mimes, and puppets. Much to my chagrin, I often got picked out of the group to participate in some silly stunt. My heart would pound when we were told to gather together in the basement for an assembly. I'd scrunch way down in my chair and hope and pray I wouldn't be noticed. I learned my lesson early. Sentinels have to be on guard at all times, ever-vigilant. I could never be certain that trouble wasn't lurking just around the corner ready to pounce.

Why didn't I just say I didn't want to go up on stage? I didn't know I had permission to say, "No thank you." I thought I had to do what "they" asked. I didn't trust others, and I didn't trust myself. I didn't trust that I could safely express my needs and rights. It was easier to hide than to deal with it straight out. It took lots of energy and time being an ever-watchful, ever-fearful sentinel.

Blue Jay Mother

My blue jay mother, consistently diligent, was on special alert during my dating years. She privately told Jim that if his desire was to have a long-term relationship with me, he would have to cultivate not acting too interested. "Connie likes a challenge. A detached approach would work much more effectively with her," she offered.

On another occasion, closer to the time of our wedding, Mother went late at night to the radio station where he worked to advise Jim against our having a baby in the next few years. Then she forged ahead and deluged him with birth control information.

Need I tell you that I was mortified when I learned of these encounters? And I was filled with shame at Mom's interference. What a tribute to Jim for his persevering in our relationship in spite of my mother's clandestine interventions.

What chores blue jays encounter! Sentinels have their work cut out for them.

Policing Adult Kids

It's a challenge for parents to give up blue jay duty for their adult children. Letting them know you love and care for them, are willing to be involved in their lives as much as you and they together agree, is a delicate balancing-act.

It was getting close to graduation and our son Jay

was not certain what he wanted to do with his college degree. He was testing the waters and working at Jim's law firm. One of the lawyers told Jay about a friend of his who was in pilot training. Jay applied. We were thrilled when he was accepted, especially Jim who was delighted that one of his sons shared his interest in flying. Jay appeared to be a natural. He was the first one in his class of those who'd never flown to get his private license.

At Thanksgiving time, Jay and Trish (who was nearly ready to be certified as an elementary teacher) became engaged. In our ducks-in-a-row mentality, we felt the kids were right on target.

However, when they returned from a visit to Trish's family, Jay announced that he was dropping out of pilot training, Trish was quitting school, they were going to move to Missouri and get married fairly soon.

Wham! Were Jim and I surprised! We had several talks with them all the while remembering the fateful talks Jim's parents had with us. We reassured the children that, no matter their final decision, we loved them both unconditionally. We just wanted them to think through—carefully—the opportunities they were leaving behind.

Jay and Trish went ahead with their plans. They married in the early spring and are living in a little trailer on the farm belonging to Trish's parents. They're busy with new dreams and plans. Fortunately, the blue jay in both Jim and me retreated to a safe perch. Jay and Trish are learning and growing together. What we can do is pray for them and wish them much love and joy on their journey. This powerful principle, detachment with love, made no sense to me before I became so ill, before my road to recovery.

Perhaps you, too, have older children. Maybe they're 30 or 40 or more. You may be struggling with your blue jay job. "Adult kids" *are* a breed apart. We are the parents; they are the children. Now that they're grown, we must recognize that it's not the parents' prerogative—nor responsibility—nor privilege—to boss these special people. Whatever we've done to encourage their growth, we've done. If we can all be adults together, what happy freedom this can bring!

To be "easy" with another, to enjoy times together with no agendas, is not only liberating but beautiful. And, ultimately, to be able to express admiration and love directly to one another would constitute some of the best interaction we can ever find on this earth.

Mates on Duty

What about mates being sentinels in one another's lives? A mate can tell you about your bad breath or that your fly is open. I've given Jim permission to be one of the blue jays in my life. Sometimes it seems a good idea, at times not. Jim was on guard duty for me the day he met Sam. Sam is my special friend. He is what is called today mentally challenged.

"When my dad got drunk, he'd hit me in the head and that's why I'm like I am," Sam confided in me one day. Sam doesn't have a driver's license, but he does have a new blue bike. One day Jim met me for lunch where Sam busses tables. Sam gave me his usual big hug. He told Jim I was his special girlfriend. "Would you like to see my new bike?" Sam asked Jim.

As we were leaving the restaurant, Jim reflected, "I wonder if you're giving Sam inappropriate messages about your friendship? Considering the way he hangs around you, maybe he doesn't understand."

"Understand what?" I demanded.

"I just think you need to be more cautious and maybe not, well, quite so friendly."

What was that supposed to mean? What was Jim getting at? Did he think I was encouraging Sam in an improper way? Oh, my—something else to cause alarm.

The next few times I had lunch at this favorite deli, I felt unsettled around Sam. I tried to be friendly, but not too friendly, whatever that means. It wasn't the same, though. I was uneasy. And I worried that Sam noticed.

Several weeks later, my friend Mary and I were sitting outside the deli having lunch. The crowd had dwindled; just a few of us were left. Sam was off in a corner, close to the sidewalk, cleaning off tables. I could see the parking area and observed an expensive car pull in. The gentleman who stepped out had obviously achieved great success by the world's standards. He had on silk tailored slacks—not a wrinkle anywhere—and an expensive shirt. He walked around the car and opened the passenger door. Out bounded an adorable, little blonde girl attired in a parochial school plaid skirt, white blouse, and loafers. She was obviously delighted to be with this man. They were holding hands as they walked up the sidewalk. I overheard her say as she looked up adoringly at him, "Daddy, I got an A on my science project. Thanks a lot for helping me. Isn't that great?" He smiled down at her and I was touched by his tenderness.

When father and daughter were nearly adjacent to Sam who had his back to them, the man stopped and gently put his other hand on Sam's shoulder.

"Hi, Sam. How are you today?" Sam turned my way to greet them and on his face was sheer delight.

"Hi, Brian. Hi, Melissa," Sam enthusiastically responded. "I'm good."

"Are you almost finished with your duties?" Brian asked.

"I will be at 2:00. It's been a pretty busy day."

"Melissa and I are so happy to see you, Sam. Do you think you could take time out and have a bite of lunch with us? I'll order for you; what would you like?" Moved to tears, I could readily see that Brian and Melissa had given Sam the most wonderful gift they could: the precious gift of themselves.

Jim's admonition was not wrong. But, in turn, I became overly cautious and reacted. Brian and Melissa didn't act or react. They just opened their hearts to Sam. How extraordinary and encouraging to witness kind, sensitive, gracious people who are not bound up in their own insecurities: people who know how to give love and receive it in return. Not only did Brian present Sam with a priceless gift, he modeled for his daughter the greatest gift of all—unequivocal, unconditional love.

Here Come the Watchmen!

Friends being blue jays for one another can be healthy. Some of my friends are blue jays in my life for the pure and simple reason that I've asked them to be. However, self-appointed watchmen are another matter. When I became desperately ill, most of these people were shocked to discover that Connie Teilborg didn't have it all together. Remember how hard I'd worked to give that appearance? Some of these folks I once thought were my friends.

Do you recall Job's accusers: Eliphaz, Bildad, and Zophar? They had all the answers to Job's suffering. If only Job would do this—or that—or whatever, he would be healed. Job's own wife tells him to curse God and die! Job's support system left much to be desired.

My blue jays were convinced they knew the reasons I was suffering and felt convicted to share them with me. *"Connie, the only way you're going to get well is to get out of that 12-step recovery program. It's not of the Lord."* And, how about these gems of wisdom:

> *"Connie, you need to stay away from all psychologists and psychiatrists—even the ones who are Christians."*
>
> *"Those 'people' are tools of the devil. You'll never get well if you keep getting advice from them. They don't know what's best for you."*
>
> *"They won't help teach you how to be dependent on the Lord."*
>
> *"Just stay away from them, all of them!"*

Support...Not Platitudes

> **When we're in distress, we need support, not platitudes. These blue jays think they know more than the other birds. They certainly don't care how offensive they are. They love to throw their weight around and flash their self-proclaimed superiority.**

Just because people have heard many sermons and read the Bible doesn't necessarily mean they understand the heart of God. They may have misinterpreted many, many passages. In their zeal, coupled with their lack of discernment, they may ramrod other people. They haven't recognized that their **opinions** don't replicate God's **wisdom**. Because they're only human, they remain that way: fallible. Such persons not only offend hurting souls, but they actually compound difficulties for others.

To study the Bible isn't the same as to study physics . . . or Russian literature . . . or calculus . . . or French. Ludicrous to think so, you might say. Why, then, the trend in some religious circles to discard everything that psychology and psychiatry offer to us? Truth—whether factual or abstract—is evident in all academic disciplines. Truth, wherever it be found, demands our attention and respect.

I've come to see that keeping myself out of harm's way is critical to my recovery process. Continually dodging the bullets of these fair-weather friends proved too exhausting and unsettling. Today, I don't share my life with them. And since I didn't and am not presently heeding their advice, they don't want to be part of it anyway. They have their hands full busily orchestrating the lives of others. It's easy to figure out their next project when you catch their pet phrase: "They're just not where we'd like them to be spiritually."

As a matter of record, not once—never at any time—did Dr. Hammerschlag undermine my faith. Just the opposite was true. He encouraged me to look to my faith, trust in my faith, grow in my faith, knowing that this was an all-important key—an integral part of my getting well.

One of the efficient and effective ways to choose a counselor is to rely on a referral from one you respect: church leader, friend, physician, family member. Charges for the initial consultation fee and follow up visits should be discussed in advance of the first session. Do not be afraid to ask questions (anything you deem pertinent) of the one you are trusting to help facilitate your healing.

Say WHAT, Dr. Hammerschlag?

Once I thought Dr. H. had overstepped his boundaries as my blue jay. Because of the complexity and persistence of my depression, Jim and I had incurred an abundance of medical bills. The statute of limitations to file suit against the medical lab was due to run out. We met with a lawyer friend of ours and discussed the circumstances of the toxic overdose with him. He said we had an excellent case and encouraged us to move forward.

When I told Dr. Hammerschlag about our plan, he shook his head. "No, Connie, I won't be a part of this.

It would not, I repeat, **not** be in your best interest to get involved in a lengthy legal battle. You're going to have to trust me on this one. Let it go."

I was incredulous! What could C.H. be thinking? How could he do this to me—to us? He knows the agony I've been going through and will, undoubtedly, continue to go through for sometime. He is aware the lab made a terrible mistake. He realizes that without his testimony, the testimony of my primary care physician, my case is dead in the water. What about all the other women who are going to that same lab and putting their lives on the line? And there might be something even more sinister than an occasional accident happening at that lab. I was heartsick about Dr. Hammerschlag's position. I thought we should blow the whistle on these people: so-called professionals who had precipitated such torment in my life.

I think Jim was somewhat relieved. As a lawyer, he understood how grueling an experience it would be for me. So . . . we let sleeping dogs lie.

How does the saying go? What goes around, comes around! Later a national TV network sent an investigative team that uncovered shoddy, incompetent work by these same lab owners and their employees. The network exposed the malpractice in a national newscast. Apparently, employees of this lab were accused of failing to detect the presence of potential cancer cells on a disturbing number of pap smear slides.

Carl Hammerschlag was right. I didn't need to be the sentinel for the lab. Blue jays with much shriller calls, much more visibility and power were on guard watching **that** forest.

Dangerous Watchmen

Do you have watchmen in your life who don't have your best interests at heart? Do you allow them to chatter raucously at you...and you continue going back for more? It is important to learn that an inability to say 'no' will often align you with people who will rarely say 'yes' to you. Saying 'no' sometimes means saying 'yes' to better things for you.

Old habits and dysfunctional ways are doggedly persistent, but slowly and surely you'll see which persons are honest sentinels for you. You'll learn to know which blue jays will bring out the best in you...and how you can encourage the finest in them.

Birds of a Feather...

Just two months before the war began in 1939, my friend Hanna Miley was one of 10,000 children whisked out of Germany via trains. Recently, she has been designated as part of the Survivors of the Shoah (holocaust) Visual History Foundation.

Making preparations for the video taping of her life story, Hanna began rummaging through a box of her memorabilia and found the round, cardboard tag, #8,814, with cord attached that had been placed around her neck directly before she boarded the train that took her to England: that remarkable train trip that spared her life.

As she was undoing the knots in the cord, Hanna was suddenly torn with the thought that, most likely, it was her dear mother, who later died in a concentration camp, who had carefully tied these time-worn knots. Hanna was overcome with emotion at the poignancy of the memory.

The crew in charge of the filming were graciously solicitous of Hanna; she was touched by their incredible sensitivity. I was intrigued to learn that the interviewer has called Hanna, at least twice, since the taping, once from New York. Hanna expressed her gratitude at the concern for her well-being. Louise, the interviewer, responded, "We would not think of coming into your home, stirring up memories only to leave you without counsel should you feel the need to process your hurt and pain."

This association has put Hanna in touch with others who have endured the same kind of distress: losing loved ones as part of the horrid slaughter of the Jews. Those involved in this endeavor understand the monumental significance of the restoration that comes from laboring with kindred spirits—untying knots—together.

Those toiling through issues of their past need to be involved with others who have experienced similar heartbreak. When old wounds are lanced and the poison released, care must be taken that reinfection does not occur. How the "care" comes will be different for everyone, but come it must!

Support Groups

At Alpha, too, preparation began for my re-entry the day I arrived. The staff knew this preparation was critical for a well-balanced program. Kevin, the designated head of this delicate endeavor, appreciated that even the slightest hint of returning home struck sheer terror in my heart. The major emphasis was geared to my continued therapy with the counselor(s) back home and the return to, or initiation into, a support group. *Support groups, support groups*—over and over again—their worth was pounded into our heads. "The quickest way to healing is spending time with those walking the same path," we were admonished.

A Safe Harbor

A safe harbor of love and confirmation is critical. Hidden somewhere in the deepest recesses of our spirit may be the thought that we're blowing our ordeal way out of proportion. Were those episodes, in actuality, as painful as we remember them? The validation that our pain is real, our recollections

are accurate as we understand them, is crucial for healing.

Many feel reluctant to seek help from support groups or counselors out of concern for the protection of parents. Maybe we've been taught, as part of our religious upbringing, that it is lofty and noble to suffer in silence. This heresy can be the death-knell to our healing.

Reach out; seek individual and group help; learn to release your fears in a safe environment. No more being locked in the cellars of your mind. Permit yourself to be unfettered and freed.

Re-entry

The closer the time came for me to leave Alpha, the more ambivalent my feelings. Inevitably, the day arrived: election day. Jim picked me up at the airport, then took me directly to our polling place to vote. No interrogation about mental hospitals from the workers. I imagined, however, while waiting in line that those around me could decode the invisible, ink message stamped across my forehead: **I've been in treatment for clinical depression!**

The first few days back home were perplexing. Dazed, I was confused about how to make choices, to go with the flow. The major rivers in my life had been dammed for a season. And now new tributaries were branching off, flowing in different directions, and I wasn't certain how to respond to these new courses. At first it seemed I was paddling upstream. As the days gradually blended into weeks, the weeks into months, I slowly became aware I was actually incorporating into my life these new life lessons that I had learned. It was cause for rejoicing!

Positive Watchfulness

The weekend after my return from Alpha, Jim had to be away. He encouraged me to invite Beverly, my roommate from Alpha, to spend the weekend with me. Jim had read about a seminar he felt would be inspirational and thought Beverly and I should go. So we went.

In short order, Beverly and I decided the speaker was in denial—big time. She used tasteless humor to cover up the painful things that had happened to her and her family. Beverly and I became more and more unsettled about the content as the speaker continued. Before the first break, this woman dispassionately related several tragic events in her life. She closed with the comment: "There were so many things going on in my life that I told a friend, 'You may have to put me in one of those 'homes' for bewildered women where they do nothing all day but make baskets.'" Chuckle—chuckle.

Beverly and I looked at one another, gathered our things together, and left. We'd just come from one of those "homes," and it hurt to have our experiences impugned. Beverly and I chose to be on guard and remove ourselves from those who would undermine our recovery process.

The Right Church

The summer of the toxic dose of estrogen I'd felt the strong desire to be affiliated with a body of believers who were truly connected to one another. With great care, the staff at Alpha chose where they took us on Sunday mornings for worship. They made certain the gospel of grace was preached and not the doctrines of legalism. I had wanted to worship where it mattered whether or not I showed up on Sunday mornings. I needed to be in a place where I could use my gifts and where I could affirm and be affirmed. Jim and I eventually decided Open Door Fellowship was the place for us.

All Just Schmucks

What's different about ODF? The shepherds are watchmen committed to the gospel of grace. They understand we all come out of some kind of woundedness. We're all struggling warriors; we're all ragamuffins. As Carl Hammerschlag says, "We're all just schmucks." However a person comes to Open Door Fellowship is fine. Just come! Broken, battered, crippled, scarred, tarnished and tattered, just come.

One of the precepts taught at ODF is based on the notion that we must magnify one another's strengths while protecting one another's weaknesses. Discerning what we each allow into our lives to encourage us in this process is essential to our individual, spiritual growth. This concept has helped me recognize and apply this truth: The Lord came to heal the sick, to mend the brokenhearted.

Honor Guards

We all require sentinels of our forest, watchmen of the day and night. We desire guards with integrity. We crave blue jays who have our best interest at heart. We yearn for watchmen who will walk with us on our journey; not ahead to dictate where we are to go; nor behind to judge us when we stumble and fall. But hand-in-hand to cry with us when we're sad or frightened; to encourage us when the road ahead is perilous; to rejoice with us in the differing sizes and shapes of our rainbows.

CHAPTER SEVEN
Blue Indigo

I Corinthians 13:12 *The glass we look through now is dark and obscure, but someday we will see things clearly—just as the Lord sees us.*

It has a melancholy aspect to it, that bluish-purplish color between late afternoon and evening. It's the time for fussy babies, frazzled nerves on long drives home from work, frantic get-the-house-picked-up/dinner-started time. Mood indigo: that feelin' that goes stealin' right down to your toes.

Many who suffer with depression find indigo to be the most difficult time of the day. For me that was true. Perhaps it was due to the tremendous energy it took to get from morning to night; to just keep going. Twilight time was insufferable—filled with my immeasurable dread at the forthcoming long night to follow. A sense of impending doom weighed me down. I was reminded of a single night long ago.

I was staying with a grade school friend whose father was the train depot manager in the tiny town of Lucerne, Colorado. I slept not a wink that night. Moments before a train was due to pass alongside the station, I heard, first faintly, then more urgently, the clattery-clack of the train on the tracks. A slight vibration followed the first hint of sound. As the mighty coal-burning engine roared closer and closer through the blackness of night, the sound mushroomed until I was certain my heart would burst with the terror of it all.

As the noise diminished, I would cautiously rise to look out the second story window of my friend's bedroom at the fading light of the caboose. When I was convinced no harm would come to me, I'd settle back down under the toasty covers close to the warmth of my friend's undisturbed body. As the gentle softness of near sleep began to envelop me, I'd hear the distant rumble of yet another approaching black monster. That night seemed an eternity!

Bittersweet Recollections

Bittersweet memories, too, are called up from our subconsciousness when it's blue indigo time. The past happiness is overlaid with a sense of loss. Childhood disappointments come back to haunt us. I sometimes muse about Blackie, my horse. He was a delight: my pride and joy.

Blackie became mine at a time when I was feeling especially fragile and lonely. He was one of the farm horses, and one day I asked my dad and Uncle Sonny if I could have him for my own. They agreed. Oh, how thrilled I was! I delighted in his shiny, black coat, and I loved how excited Blackie was to see me when I ran home from school to feed him.

Dashing home one late, indigo afternoon, I was surprised to find Blackie was not in the pasture. My dad and uncle were fixing fences and I hurried to ask, "Where's Blackie?" They appeared reluctant to comment. Finally Uncle Sonny said, "Uh, well, he's gone."

"Gone, gone where?" I exclaimed anxiously.

"We sold him," answered Dad.

I cried, "You mean he's really gone, gone for good? He can't be gone! You mean gone forever? You wouldn't do that! Sell Blackie! Why? He was **my** horse!" I ran to the house as fast as my legs could carry me. I sobbed for hours.

Much later, I learned that Dad and Uncle Sonny had hoped to sell another horse. When the prospective buyers came to look, they were drawn to Blackie and made an offer to buy him: an offer my dad and uncle didn't refuse.

New Eyes

> **How often have I caused pain in my own sons' lives, inadvertently, by my need for undue control, expediency, or my unwillingness to examine my actions from their perspective? There are "monster" parents, of course, who knowingly inflict pain—physical and emotional—on their children. Most of us do not fall into that category; we come to our interactions with our children believing we are choosing the "right" way. In actuality, we're inflicting wounds that may last a lifetime.**

You may think that long-standing ways of interaction cannot be modified. It's never too late to make living amends to our children. We can start today asking their forgiveness for the suffering we caused and adopting an open willingness to see in a new way, through different eyes, their eyes.

The King's Answer

Shortly before I was first hospitalized, during a session with Dr. Hammerschlag I'd tried to put into words the agony I was feeling, tried to explain the anguish of my pain. It was physical as well as emotional. I'd read about the phantom pain amputees experience. That's how I would characterize what I was experiencing. The pain was physically real, but not in any specific spot, sort of free floating. It appeared simultaneously everywhere and nowhere: excruciating, agonizing, paralyzing pain.

My brain was in such anguish that my head hurt. Carl Hammerschlag reclined into his story-telling mode and began a saga. I was attempting to follow him as he rambled on and on.

A distraught King was frantic to find the answer to the emotional suffering he'd been experiencing for years. The finest healers in the land had been summoned, but not a single one was able to help the King with the pain in his head. He would have paid handsomely for an answer, but to no avail.

One day a simple peasant was admitted to the King's court and declared he could guide the King to one who knew the secret that would end the King's mental torture.

"I can take you to the wisest man in the world," stated the peasant. "You must accompany me on this journey. It is a difficult trip, King, and you must prepare for many hardships."

"Take me to him. Oh, do take me to him!" implored the King. "I will do anything—go anywhere—to find the answer that will stop this pain in my head."

It was a long, tedious, often arduous journey. At long last the King and peasant climbed the final mountain of their destination. Buried within the mountain was a tiny cave. Inside the cave was a strange, sprite-like little man: the wisest man in the world.

Indeed! thought the King. *How could this curious creature know the answer to my sufferings? I've come all this way for nothing. But now that I'm here, I might as well listen to what he has to say.*

"Tell me. Tell me the answer to this torment I feel," pleaded the King.

The wisest man in the world looked at the King. With great compassion and with wisdom in his eyes and voice, he responded. "Your answer, dear, fine King, is a simple one. It's the answer to all life's questions, great and small: THIS TOO SHALL PASS. It will pass, indeed."

What a ridiculous story! I felt like the King must have felt. Dr. H. used all this valuable time to relate this ludicrous story that ends with, "This Too Shall Pass."

"A crisis of faith!" C.H. called it. It's when you believe that your faith can no longer sustain you; when you've lost all hope; when you believe, with all your heart, that "it" will never pass.

Will It Pass?

For you who have walked this journey, you know there is truth in these four words: "THIS TOO SHALL PASS." Perhaps there are those of you reading this who do not believe it is so. You are experiencing your very own "crisis of faith." It's a frightening place to be, how well I know.

I was still in the midst of "the crisis" that indigo, early evening at Alpha. It was my third evening there and I continued to entertain thoughts of ending my life. We'd just finished dinner and were sitting outside around the pool. Our medications arrived by messenger boy each evening at dusk. Darting in through the back gate came the young man with his delivery. Suddenly Kelly jumped up and shrieked, "Did you see that? In he bursts through that gate like he owned the place. Why, anybody could do that—some rapist, ax-murderer, whoever, whatever. This is a dangerous place. I thought I'd be safe here, but I'm not. You guys aren't either;

none of us is. We'd better report this and get a big lock on that gate."

In short order, Kelly had nearly everyone fired up. I sat quietly thinking. The idea began to form in my mind. Certainly murder would be a simple solution to my complex problems. I had many rough days, weeks, months, perhaps even years ahead of me. If someone were to come through the back gate and kill me, that would take care of everything. I wouldn't have to fret about whether or not suicide is an unforgivable sin. All the agony would be gone.

Next morning in Group, I shared my thoughts. Mark burst out laughing. "Your small step from suicide to homicide is not a giant leap for you or womankind, Connie. The only giant step for you would be in the wrong direction, like over a cliff." So much for that. When would these thoughts end; would I ever be free from them?

Anger Work

Kelly and I took a late afternoon walk the beginning of my second week at Alpha. A few days earlier, we'd happened on a wrecked, rusted, abandoned car in the weeds on the side of the mountain.

"Hey, let's go beat up on that old car," I suggested to Kelly. We found a circuitous path leading us above the car. Eagerly, we gathered a pile of rocks. One by one, taking turns, we pelted the car as we named people and things that caused us anger. No need for The Colorado Rockies to send their scouts. Only about 25 percent of the time did we strike the car. It felt good hearing the bang! bang! After we'd spent our energy, we walked farther up the hill and found a large rock to sit on. Below was a lovely neighborhood street nestled at the foot of the mountain. We fantasized that we were little girls again and that we lived in that safe-looking cul-de-sac. It was a good indigo time. We were on the road to healing. We were on the right road.

Where's the Progress?

When a person slips into mood indigo, she is reminded again of three steps forward, two steps back. Sometimes it seems there's been no progress.

Jim and I were going to be in Colorado and thought we'd try to see my parents. I'd phone them from our cabin.

Near dusk, I called them.

"Hello," I heard my mom say.

"Hi, Mom. It's Connie."

"Hello, hello."

"Mom, it's Connie," louder this time.

"I said hello, is someone there?" It was evident to me that I could hear her but she couldn't hear me. I thought I'd give it one last try.

"Mom, Mom, can you hear me?"

"Well, whoever is on this line, don't you know it's

very rude to call someone and not say anything? What I do if I get the wrong number is say, 'Please excuse me, I have the wrong number.' That's what I do and it wouldn't hurt you to do the same thing. You are just very rude to stay on the phone. I can hear that you are still on the phone."

About this time I could hear my dad yelling in the background, "D--n it to h--l, Lucile. Just hang up the d--n phone! Don't just stay on there like some fool. They're just a bunch of 'rubber-neckers' anyway; that's what they are. I told you to hang up the d--n phone."

Slowly, I placed the receiver back in the cradle. My heart was racing. I was trembling all over. I sat down on the bed and wept. I felt despondent, discouraged, and a touch shamed. I had this overwhelming desire to do what I'd always wanted to do from the time I can remember. I wanted to say, *Please stop fighting. Won't you please stop and be kind to one another?* And I wanted them to notice that I was there, that it wasn't just about them. It was about all of us, the whole family.

So…I was on the other end, the receiving end, like I'd always been. Mom and Dad didn't even know it. They were simply responding the way they'd always done; making it all about them. It was fifty years ago replayed. Mom expending useless energy being the sentinel in someone's life she didn't even know she knew. And Dad raving at her because she didn't do it the way he wanted her to.

Actually, I had to both cry and chuckle a bit. After the abortive phone call, I fixed myself some tea and went out on the back porch. The sun was just setting. And I remembered how the sun had **almost** set in my life. I remembered that today, before the exchange with my parents, I had been at peace. I knew that the moment of shame I had felt was not mine to feel. I was aware that there—but for the grace of God—go I. Yes, I could easily have chosen to travel the same road my parents had traveled with nothing new under the sun, doing the same old things in the same old ways.

Recapping the Journey

After my stay at Alpha, I recognized it was time for me to start practicing what I'd learned. I was continuing to see Dr. Hammerschlag on a weekly basis. It was early December; Dr. H. asked me if I wanted to take a walk during our session. His home is situated at the foot of Camelback Mountain, a beautiful setting. The days were getting shorter. It was nearly sunset—indigo time. We walked to the east. The reflection of the sun off the mountain displayed the most striking color: a dramatic indigo. It felt good, just the two of us walking together in the late afternoon exchanging stories. I heard something behind me and turned to look.

"You know, Connie, if we focus on what's behind us, we'll see only where we've been. For a season it's good to know where we've been. You've experienced that season. Now it's time to look forward, to look ahead, to see where you're going."

The Black Claw

Another time, while I was relating more of my Alpha experiences to Dr. Hammerschlag, the ubiquitous candle on his table began smoldering. Dreadful, black smoke dramatically crept toward me—a sinister, black claw reaching down to grab me so like the black claw I had drawn at Alpha when I was asked to "picture" my depression.

C.H. observed as I recoiled in alarm and demanded, "What's happening? What's going on?"

"This looks just like the black claw coming back to get me again!" I cried as I watched the black smoke, tears filling my eyes. Dr. Hammerschlag quietly responded,

"Look again, Connie. Look carefully. What do you see now?" As I watched, the smoke curled into a strange, yet distinct scroll-like form.

"It looks like a scroll now, no longer like a claw," I barely breathed.

"Isn't that interesting?" Dr. H. remarked. "What at first glance was so alarming to you has changed form and now presents itself 'scroll-like.' You are to learn from this blackness. Isn't that what you are coming to understand from the darkness of your depression? And you are learning significant and crucial life-lessons."

Out of the Ordinary

Is your journey through the rainbow causing you to see many things in wholly new ways? Moses, in the Old Testament, took off his shoes when God spoke to him at the burning bush. Why was this necessary? For Moses to see things in a new way, he had to step out of the ordinary, his everyday shoes, and be willing to see in an extraordinary way. In your life, walking boldly through the bands of the rainbow, stepping out of the ordinary, can lead to splendid insights adding glorious new shades of color to your life and the lives you touch.

CHAPTER EIGHT
Violets

Matthew 11:28	*I will grant you blessed rest if you turn to me with your weariness and burdens.*

Each time I observe the gentle beauty of the last band of the rainbow, I am reminded of the relaxed loveliness of violets: my friend Gerry's favorite flower. Gerry likes violets because they like her. . . . Violets are low maintenance, not like roses, for example. You have to be careful when you pick roses or you'll get pierced. You can get punctured just arranging them. If you grow roses, you have to dust them, feed them, prune them.

Not violets. Violets don't like you to fiddle with them too much. They have a simple, oval leaf that is slightly soft—like the little fuzzy caterpillars that you barely dared touch with your pointer finger when you were little. Violets have no sharpness to hurt you; nothing that will pierce your heart or puncture your balloon. There's no subterfuge in them. They are what they are. Their loose spray of flowers spells freedom, relaxation, tranquility. They're not all caught up in their "doing." They know how to just "be."

Violets were the favorite flower of Gerry's mother. Growing up in Minnesota, Gerry and her sisters would venture out, after the first thaw in the spring, to find wild violets to bring to their mother. Imagine such a fragile-looking flower able to withstand the Minnesota winters!

Gerry has a violet plant in her Phoenix garden that a man gave her more than 30 years ago. Imagine this beautiful flower being able to withstand the Arizona summers!

One should look closely at the violet's leaves and stems. It's comforting to see those delicate, vibrant, little flowers resting in such sturdy stock. I think that's the way it's supposed to be with God and us. We can rest in His care knowing that He will support and protect us.

As lovely as the violet flowers, and as vital the stems and leaves, this plant couldn't survive without a strong root system. It's the root system—the solid grounding—that, ultimately, makes all the difference. For me, it's the belief in something greater than myself. It's the security of knowing I have roots to support me. It's the reality that God is God and I am not. When the winds and rains come, as they do and will, I have no need to fear. I'm tucked safely in His loving arms. I won't be blown apart by the wind.

I was fortunate that my root system was still intact—an amazing fact since I hadn't fed or watered it for many years. Yet, that's the way it is with God. He'd been there all the time waiting for me to come to Him and ask for help. And the only way I could come to that place of need was to be confronted with something I couldn't fix myself.

When I ultimately believed with all my heart that I was secure in His arms; when I believed I wouldn't be torn apart by the wind or submerged in the flood; then, and only then, was it safe for me to grow. Growing means change and change involves growing. It's not a dichotomy to rest and grow at the same time. Violets do that. It's a tranquil growing—a stretching and changing—a willingness to come to things in a fresh way. It's a "be still and know that I am God."

A Precious Violet

Actually, long ago my Grandma Anderson began helping me set down a few roots in my life. We lived in the same yard with her. Grandma and I were kindred spirits. She knew all about me; she was aware when I needed her most. More often than not, after I'd been punished for being naughty, she'd come to our front door and ask me to go along with her to gather eggs.

Those times were priceless. I remember how my hand felt in hers. I remember how her dresses brushed up against my cheek as she tenderly held my head close to her body. I remember how delighted she was when I skipped along beside her. When I got a bit older and there was trouble at home, I'd run next door to her. She'd stop whatever she was doing, gather me to her, cradle my head against her breast, and let me cry and cry until my tears were spent.

This extraordinary woman helped her father raise her four younger brothers and sisters when their mother died. She married and had five children to care for. Her husband, Grandfather Karl, died in his 50's leaving her responsible for the farm and all that was involved with its operation. Then along came a little, blond-haired granddaughter who was emotionally fragile and desperately in need of someone to cherish her. Grandma Anderson loved me unconditionally. She was God's special violet gift to me.

Timely Lessons

Later on, Gerry entered my life when I needed her most. She has the gift of noticing the beauty around her without being 'so heavenly minded she's no earthly good.' She's one of the wise women in my life. Like the violet, she's strong and secure in who and what she is. This stability allows her to be soft, gentle, patient, and kind with those around her. With me!

Time Wasters

I've learned important lessons from Gerry and from other close friends. For a people-pleaser like me, it's been a struggle to ask myself this question:

Why waste my time and theirs if I'm not interested?

Frequently, we allow whoever happens to be around to latch on to us as a friend. We forget that life is short and that friendship is more than hanging out with casual acquaintances. We can choose our close friends wisely. With these individuals, we will be mutually concerned about spiritual and emotional growth. When we come to that fork in the road, where we all inevitably arrive, we desire those around us who will help us choose the better way—better for our growth and the growth of our loved ones. A true friend is one who will say the hard things to you knowing that the friendship may momentarily suffer, but that your highest and best self will be fostered and nourished.

Friendship requires a special chemistry in order to sustain it. When someone wants to spend more time with you than you do with her, it doesn't necessarily indicate you don't like her. You simply don't feel connected; the relationship lacks zest. Consider freeing that person up so you can both move on and make more intimate friendships.

We can attempt to have too many close friends. There's only so much of us to be divided and spread around. If we have two or three intimate friends, we are blessed. Friendships require time and nurturing. If you have more than a handful, someone's getting shortchanged—probably you.

A Short Reply

Another strong but kind violet lesson allows a person to reply,

"I won't be able to. . . . That won't work out for me."

That's all! No reasons! For those of us who have shame issues in our background, we don't feel a simple "no" is sufficient. So . . . we ramble: "I really wish we could come for dinner but my second cousin twice removed from Pakistan has a nephew in Connecticut whose wife is having a baby and they have no one to look after their three-year-old. So I offered on the second Tuesday of every month to take the child to McDonalds then to Jump and Play afterward."

On and on we go, ad nauseam. All we need to say… "That's not going to work for me, but thanks for the thought." That's all—just quit!

Forgive Me

Gentle people who have laid down strong roots can say,

"I'm sorry; please forgive me."

They say it quickly; they save lots of anguish. Keep short lists. In the whole scheme of things, does it really matter who said what and when he said it? There is always a part of the disagreement/misunderstanding that you can own. It is our stubborn pride that wants to make certain we get the last word, prove the other person wrong.

Keep the messages limited to "I," and take care not to get into the other's inventory. "I'm so sorry I hurt you. Please forgive me." It's as simple as that!

Integrity

Others have taught me that a sincere friend will,

Always, always, always tell the truth!

When directly asked, you must directly answer with the truth. Truth and love go hand in hand. To fail to be truthful is to inhibit your own and another's spiritual growth. It means you don't change a few "minor" details when relating a story someone told you. It's about integrity.

How you tell the truth is another matter. You don't have to unload the whole truck of truth on everyone. If telling the truth is done with kindness, and, more importantly, motivated by love, it will bring about change—change that will enhance the life of the giver as well as the receiver.

You probably recall the little saying: "You aren't what you think you are. You aren't what others think you are. You are what you think others think you are."

Often, we're so preoccupied with presenting an image of ourselves that we don't even know who the real "me" is. A big part of telling the truth is knowing who you are. What are my strengths? What are my weaknesses? What are the areas of my life that put me in harm's way—places where I feel I have to be or say something I'm not—where I am compelled to lie? We value in others their ability to be forthright. It's refreshing and honorable. They, too, will respect us for our openness and honesty.

Caregiving vs. Caretaking

It's a violet truth that the difference between caregiving and caretaking is the difference between healthy and unhealthy thinking. Caregiving reaches out in love and encouragement to foster in the recipient healthiness and wholeness. Caretaking extracts from the healing process; taking from people their responsibility to change and grow.

> **How arrogant we are to consider we know best how other human beings should think and behave! Rather than trying to change their actions, we should change our reactions. Our own life's journey should challenge us sufficiently enough so that we have no time, nor inclination, to meddle in the lives of others.**

That Special Person

The lessons continue. I can see Gerry doesn't work so hard at doing life. She doesn't return, over and over again, to unhealthy and destructive people, nor to unhealthy and destructive behavior. She doesn't have to experience dysentery to know she doesn't want it. And you and I don't want it, either! We're after the gold: the peace, the joy.

> **Lucky you if you've found a friend who patiently waits to encourage you when you come crawling back licking your wounds after having gone off on some tangent.**
>
> **Such a friend won't explode with, "I'm sick of you and sick of your behavior! Why don't you get a clue about how to act?"**
>
> **Maybe this friend is nothing like you, and perhaps that's good. This special person waits for you to grow, to learn to trust the Lord. And while she's waiting, she reflects on the rainbow—the beauty of the journey.**

Searching for Joy

Before I had learned some important violet concepts, I truly believed I would never experience joy again. I longed for contentment. I wanted to know and to feel that all would be well in my spirit.

The thrill of a roller coaster ride…the merriment of seeing Santa Claus…the pleasure of a fine meal…the happy tears when greeting a loved one…the fun of a day at Disneyland… These times add important dimensions to our lives. But the deep-seated, quiet, confident joy that comes when an individual is at peace with God, and has peace within, is something much different.

Biblical Truth

Many verses in the Bible teach the concept that joy can be permanent when an individual recognizes dependence on the Lord. Such joy does not come and go depending on circumstances. Rather, obedience to God's commands leads to more trust and hope. Romans 15:13 tells us that God, the Author of hope, can fill us with peace and joy if we rely on Him. Yes, we can spill over with precious hope.

That heartfelt sense of well-being that I had sought so long began to evidence itself the more I recovered. I was becoming aware, once more, that God is God and I am not! I, in turn, could relax, and open my violet self to the glorious possibilities of living life with joy.

Lovely, lovely violets! Just looking at them rests a weary soul. What a reminder—with their sturdy stock and deep roots—of our Lord, Who promises: "Come to Me, all who are weary and heavy-laden, and I will give you rest."

Chapter Eight: Violets

CHAPTER NINE
Revisiting the Colors

Psalm 4:1 *Indeed, it is true, Lord. You have caused me to grow through my trials.*

As you and I are joyfully revisiting the colors of our individual rainbows, we are no longer regarding black as an agent of despair. . . . We are pulling out of the morass of depression. We are allowing the dark times to be a catalyst for enlightenment.

Detaching Appropriately

When Monica, my head nurse at Alpha, stayed calm, cool, and collected during our painful encounter with Fred, the insurance representative, I asked her how she had maintained her remarkable poise.

"Well, it's a long story," Monica began. "In a nutshell, though, I will tell you that I was severely abused as a child. My father was an alcoholic, and, when it suited him, he would drape me over the toilet and beat me with his belt. He never failed to count out 100 lashes. Usually by the time he got between 40 and 50, the pain would become so unbearable that my mind fragmented into other personalities. I've attempted suicide and been in mental hospitals several times. So I've learned, in difficult situations, to detach. A big part of my recovery has been to differentiate between detaching and fragmenting. With God's help, I'm becoming whole."

For some individuals, life's journey is hard and wearisome. It takes longer to see improvement.... The lovely shades of the rainbow appear muted.... But the difficult process of recovery is worth the struggle.

Detaching Is Not Suppressing

We should remind ourselves, again and again, that the truth is closer to what we feel than to what we think. We ignore this concept to our own peril. Through a graphic story, Dr. Hammerschlag taught me:

People don't fake it till they make it;
they fake it till they die.

"Your spirit, Connie, is like the Dead Sea." The Dead Sea: The saltiest body of water in the world located at the mouth of the River Jordan. In the Middle Ages, travelers reported that no birds flew over the Dead Sea because the air there was poisonous. Today we know that birds avoid the Dead Sea because no fish are in it and little plant life can grow because of the saltiness of the water. The River Jordan flows into it from the north through a rapidly descending valley. Smaller streams also empty into the sea. This fresh water evaporates in the extreme heat in the Dead Sea basin. Thus the level of the water changes very little, and the sea never grows less salty because there is no outlet.

C. H. declared, "Your body knows it's in agony. Your brain says, 'Pull it together, don't show how you feel, be tough.' Stress hormones kick in and weaken your system. You need to cry the truth of what you feel. Instead, you squelch your emotions and let fear control you. Utimately, your body pays the price."

THINKING you're moving quickly to eradicate the blackness from your life doesn't necessarily mean you're making progress. Don't deceive yourself. What are you FEELING? What is the cry of your heart? Call out to God and receive the help you need.

Perhaps you can say with the Psalmist:

Why art thou cast down, O my soul? and why art thou disquieted in me? hope thou in God: for I shall yet praise him for the help of his countenance (Psalm 42:5 KJV).

As we praise, as we find joy . . . we'll let the bands of the rainbow contract and expand as they will. We'll revisit the colors in new, fresh ways, enjoying their frequent merging.

New Hues

RED will change from forcing my own plans to embracing God's perfect plan.

This vivid hue will bleed into forthright ORANGE as things that were formerly only mockery are replaced by the legitimate, the real.

The old, rigid rows of YELLOW will gradually brighten into the sunshine of freedom.

And, as GREEN changes from fear to faith, the mellowing with yellow will often depict our own relaxed growth. Fears, both justifiably horrible and laughingly silly, will diminish.

"Batting" Fear Away

It was late afternoon. The sky was a gorgeous, indigo color when I arrived at the cabin. It had been a difficult trip with lots of traffic. "Everybody and their dog must be trying to get out of the desert heat," I muttered to myself as I hauled my carload of things inside. Taking a few items down to the basement, I left the front and back doors open. The sky was darkening as I trudged in with my last load. I locked the doors, turned on the outside lights, and fixed myself a light supper. Nighttime settled in, as did I.

I think I'll take a warm bath and head up to the loft to watch a movie, I decided. I chose *Sound of Music*, and was singing "The Hills Are Alive with the Sound of Music" at the top of my lungs, accompanying Julie

Andrews when I caught a glimpse of a giant moth floating across the TV screen. Wow, what a huge moth; I've never seen a moth that big! That was a moth, wasn't it? What else could it be? What in heaven's name **was** that? Suddenly, it flew back across the screen and landed on the back of the couch mere inches from me. "Ahhhhhh. Oh no! Oh, pleeeeeease no. Not a bat!"

Imitating Julie Andrews, I flew down the stairs with wings on my feet. Not in joy though, but in sheer, unadulterated terror. I ran into the bedroom, slammed and locked the door. My heart was pounding! Whatever would I do? I hunkered down on the bed until my heart calmed a bit. I decided the only judicious thing was to call Jim. He'd bail me out.

"Jim, I have an emergency!"

"What's wrong?"

"Well, you see . . . it's like this. When I got here, it was getting dark so I left the doors open to take things down to the basement, and, well, then I guess I didn't think about anything flying in the cabin so I put stuff away and had supper and took a bath and went to the loft to watch a movie but during the movie this thing that I thought was a giant moth flew across the TV screen (breath-breath) but it really wasn't a giant moth after all—it was a huge bat—I think it must be the biggest bat in the whole wide world and I'm terrified."

Occasionally I exaggerate, especially if I'm overwrought. Jim attaches a more basic label: lying!

"Where are you now?"

"I'm in the bedroom with the door locked."

"Well. . . . You'll be safe enough there. Just go to sleep and try to find the bat in the morning."

"I can't just—like—go to sleep. I mean this is a really scary thing. Anyway, the movie's still on and all the lights are on in the rest of the cabin."

"I'm sure you'll be fine. Just go upstairs, shut off the movie, and the lights. Anyway, it's an 'old wives' tale—bats attacking people. They don't get caught in your hair or do any of those things you've heard about."

"I can't do that. I'm really afraid. I can't go back upstairs with 'him' flying all around."

Trying to be patient, Jim instructed, "Just put the phone down, go upstairs, and shut everything off. I'll stay on the line."

I put down the phone, steeled my nerves, then ran as fast as I could to shut off everything. Back to the bedroom I scurried.

"I did it!" I excitedly exclaimed.

"Well," he sighed. "Try to get a decent night's sleep." Needless to say, I hardly slept a wink.

No sign of the bat the next morning. I had to go into town for groceries. But first, I exhaustedly sank into the chair by the fireplace and pleaded, "Lord, you know how afraid I am. I'm sure there must be some reason You created bats, but I know the reason is **not** for them to be in my cabin. Please, please do something!"

I had my eyes closed, and as I opened them, lo and behold! Inching across the tile in front of the fireplace was the dreaded creature. Why is that bat crawling? He must be sick. He probably has rabies. Only a rabid bat would crawl. What will I do?

"Ohhhhhhhhhhh!" In a wild frenzy, I sprung out of the chair, grabbed the broom, and smashed it down as ferociously as I could on the bat. To make certain he (of course, it was a he) was dead, I did it again and then once again. Trembling from head to toe, I sat in the chair for an eternity to collect myself. When I'd stopped shaking, I cautiously lifted the broom and looked at the bat.

What a frightening sight! He looked like a miniature demon with his translucent wings, pointy little ears, and teeth that came to a sharp point. Yuck!

The next few days I busied myself putting steel wool in any cracks and crevices I could find in the cabin structure. I was convinced we'd have no more bats in the cabin. All's well that ends well, or so I stupidly thought.

A few weeks later, my friends Carolyn and Lynda came to spend a few days with me at the cabin. As is my penchant, I gave them a blow-by-blow account of the night with the bat. "But don't worry. There won't be any others because I've filled up all the holes. Anyway, this one got in when I left the doors open at twilight time."

At 3:00 the next morning, Carolyn, who was sleeping in the loft, came clamoring down the stairs squealing, "A bat! A bat just hit me in the face!"

Not again! The three of us spent the next two hours with a net on a large pole trying to capture the 'demon creature' as it flew back and forth along the logs in the highest part of the ceiling. Finally Lynda (the littlest one of us) snared it in the net. We released the bat outside and were awake for most of the rest of the night, our nerves frayed, giggling and carrying on.

We had a grate installed over the chimney. We determined that's how the bats had got in.

I've now learned that individual bats catch hundreds of night-flying insects hourly. They are essential to the balance of nature. Now, at twilight time, I watch the bats begin their nightly stealth hunt. I can thank God for them. . . . The fear is gone.

A Tranquil Spirit

As we mature, BLUE will no longer represent hypervigilence but quiet encouragement and tranquility of spirit.

And, when blue blends with INDIGO, we'll witness changes from overwhelming melancholy to optimistic potentiality. Annie, one of the patients at Alpha, is a poignant example of such growth.

Annie's Miracle

Annie is a victim of satanic, ritualistic abuse. When she arrived at Alpha, she brought her doll, Little Annie, with her. Under her bed the doll was thrust the moment Annie set foot into her bedroom at Alpha. Annie was fragile, wounded, and immensely vulnerable.

She'd just finished her individual session and came to see Kelly and me. "I have a favor to ask you guys," she tearfully stammered.

"Sure, go ahead," Kelly encouraged.

"Well, Mark thinks it's time to take Little Annie out from under the bed. I told him I couldn't do it; I told him Little Annie was just for decoration. I told him I didn't know how to be a good mother. What if I hurt Little Annie the way my parents hurt me?" By this time tears were streaming down Annie's face. I held out my arms, and she slumped into them.

As Annie sobbed, Kelly cautioned, "If you take Little Annie out from under the bed, you'll have to be really committed to taking care of her. She's your responsibility. It's a big decision, Annie. Do you think you're ready for it?"

Annie pathetically replied, "I don't know? Maybe I can do it if you guys help me and show me how to care for her. Mark said it was O.K. to ask the two of you to help. Will you? Will you baby-sit for her sometimes if I need you to?" We assured her we would.

The three of us sat quietly together waiting for Annie

to decide. Finally, she was ready to get Little Annie out from under the bed. We went to Annie's room, shut the door, and sat on the floor next to her bed. We waited while Annie cried even more. Finally, she scooted herself over as close to the bed as she could. Then, slowly and cautiously, Annie reached under the bed. Out came Little Annie. Kelly and I moved in closer. Annie limply held the doll. Kelly took Annie's arms and secured them around Little Annie. We waited. Kelly started praying quietly. Annie held her doll a little more tightly. Softly I started singing a praise song. Annie began rocking her baby. When I'd finished the song, Annie said, "That's the song I was just thinking of before you started singing it." A miracle took place that indigo afternoon.

As we progressively appreciate that God is God and we are not, we will be smitten with awe at His workings. Any shrinking VIOLET tendency will be transformed into gentle strength as we learn to rest in God's plans for us.

Simple Violet Truths

David and his wife, Shirley, direct the newcomers' class at their church. They'd planned an end-of-the-class retreat in the mountains. At the men's separate session Friday night, David observed that Paul, whom David didn't know well, appeared to be unsettled about being there. He had a disgruntled look on his face through most of David's presentation. At break time David approached Paul and asked him if he was uneasy, if there was something bothering him. "There sure is," declared Paul. "I don't believe any of this God stuff. I've come along this weekend because my wife, Sally, wanted me to, but I don't believe what you're saying, any of it!"

"Can we talk after the next session, Paul. Maybe I can help clear some things up. Would you be willing to do that?"

"Actually I was thinking of leaving, but I guess I could wait for a little while longer." During the next portion of the program David observed Paul becoming increasingly agitated as the hours wore on.

Later, over coffee, David inquired, "Tell me a bit about yourself, Paul. When and how did you decide there is no God?"

"Well, it was during Nam and I don't really want to talk about it. But that's when I found out there is no God."

"I could say a lot to you, Paul. But I won't. Will you let me pray with you and ask God to reveal Himself to you in a supernatural way this weekend?"

"Uh, well, I guess so, but it won't make a difference. Sally prays all the time and it doesn't change anything."

"Dear Heavenly Father, You know Paul, and You know all about him. He's hurting and he's confused.

Show Yourself to him this weekend. Amen. See you in the morning, Paul?"

"Don't count on it. I still may head out of here tonight."

In the early hours of the morning a member of the leadership team knocked on the door of David's cabin. He announced that Paul was loading his things into his car and getting ready to leave. David got dressed and went out to Paul's car. "You're really intent on leaving, then?" asked David.

"Yeah. I don't see much point in hanging around."

"You know, Paul, I'm feeling sad for Sally that you're leaving and you won't be driving back to Phoenix together. Won't you reconsider, for Sally's sake, and finish out the morning with us?" Paul decided to stay.

During breakfast David was told that someone would have to fill in for the speaker who'd had an emergency in Phoenix. David asked Daniel to share his "story" as the closure for the retreat.

It was a happy setting. New friends had been made, stories had been shared, and most were in a festive mood. Not Paul! Preliminaries were taken care of and then David introduced Daniel.

Daniel talked about how he had come to know the Lord. He'd pretty much done things in his own strength and in his own way until he went to Viet Nam. He'd piloted a helicopter and his aircraft was downed in a rice paddy. His co-pilot was killed. Somehow, Daniel managed to pull himself out of the chopper. He was badly injured and probably would have died right there but for the heroic efforts of the co-pilot of another helicopter that was down. "This guy rescued me from the wreckage. I guess they took him to another hospital. I don't even know his name. I told God, 'If You see me through this, I'll start paying You more attention.'" Daniel went on to say he'd spent many months in the hospital recovering and getting to know God better. His closing comment, "And there's a guy out there, somewhere, who saved my life—**twice**. Thanks buddy, from the bottom of my heart!"

And, at that moment, Paul stood up. In a quivering voice, he said, "CJAJT," the call numbers on the helicopter he'd been co-piloting that day. That same day in Viet Nam he'd pulled Daniel from his wreckage—from physical and spiritual wreckage—from death to life. Daniel stared at Paul incredulously. Paul, with tears rolling down his cheeks, looked at Daniel. Then the two of them ran joyfully to meet one another half-way with hugs and tears.

One black day in Viet Nam two helicopters were shot down. Paul saved Daniel's life that day. The fact is God heard David's simple, violet prayer. And Daniel's prayer. . . . And a prayer from Paul's heart: a simple, violet prayer, a prayer Paul didn't even know was there.

CHAPTER TEN
Gold: The Prize

Psalm 19:9-10	*The Lord rules with truth and righteousness. His proclamations shines brighter than the finest gold.*

Ah! There it is! That pot of gold at the end of the rainbow overflowing with glistening coins. I must hurry ...scoop those shiny pieces off the ground...snatch them before anyone else comes. How much will I get? I'll count my hoard in secret. Oh! It looks like pirate treasure! What can I buy? Where shall I go? What have I always wanted?

The King Midas syndrome: It is seizing the gold, sitting at the garish, gold table, stacking the piles, then counting it, over and over again. Is there enough? No, no! More must be collected and stacked and counted. What if a pile starts to dwindle? Horror of horrors! More grabbing, wrenching, yanking, straining. More! More!! More!!! Never enough.

In any rainbow illustration the kettle is always black. Why? Unwittingly or not, perhaps the big, black pot depicts man's grubby, evil intention to have it all...to not spread it around. With gluttonous greed, people clutch wildly at their elusive dreams, their pots at the end of the rainbow.

Why do we human beings lust for the seemingly unobtainable? for the quick fix? We think we know what we want. The old adage: "Say what you mean, and mean what you say," is good advice as far as it goes. Often, though, we have little awareness of WHAT we mean, let alone what we SAY.

We search and yet don't really expect to find. We buy multiple lottery tickets . . . enter sweepstakes with millions-to-one odds. This mad trip we call life renders us psychologically helpless and spiritually bereft.

It's MINE!

Maybe this unseemly grasping comes from the fear that a person won't ever 'get his.' People suffering from this scarcity mentality just know there won't be enough good things to go around. So they keep their stash closely guarded and exhibit all manner of unbecoming, selfish behavior.

Scarcity mentality can cause people to hoard not just money, but to avoid sharing an important, life-changing experience. Fear of what others might think of us if they knew what we've done or where we've been leads to stinginess. Although it was potentially embarrassing to reveal that I'd been in a recovery center for depression and had spent many months in psychiatric therapy, I knew I must. . . . The journey has not been for me alone.

You and I alike are comprehending that all that glitters is not gold. Gold doesn't tarnish, leave ugly, green-black stains. And it's not a gigantic stash of things at the end of the rainbow.

Counterfeit Gold

- **It's not—Loving things and using people.**
- **It's not—What's mine is mine and what's yours is mine, too.**
- **It's not—I'm so glad I'm not like them.**
- **It's not—I have all the answers.**
- **It's not—They did this to me so I'll do this to them.**
- **It's not—They're not where I'd like them to be spiritually.**
- **It's not—Everything's fun, fuzzy, and tip-toeing through the tulips.**
- **It's not—Everything's sad and serious and solemn.**

Cleaning Out the Debris

Not until we've experienced and lived through blackness, the darkest of times, can we fully appreciate the brilliance of the gold. The blacker the experience, the more magnificent the gold. The contrast reminds me of the August I'd watched the Forest Service stack piles of brush and limbs for the annual controlled burn. What exactly was going to happen? I'd never seen 'the burn,' since I'm usually back in Phoenix by the time it takes place.

I had grocery shopping to do. On my way to town, I noted that the fires had been started. It was fascinating seeing all those blazes smack dab in the middle of the forest. I wondered how the Forest Service could be absolutely, positively certain that there would be no "runaways."

I was in town longer than I'd planned and was returning home. The piles were nearly burned up with an abundance of black smoke coming from them. At one point the smoke was so thick I could see little in front of me. I slowed to a snail's pace thinking I might have to stop the car.

When I'm in the car traveling alone, I often talk out loud to myself. This was one of those occasions. "Well, this is pretty stupid. The Forest Service has obviously lit too many fires. This is really dangerous. What if someone is speeding behind me? He couldn't see me until it was too late. He'd hit me for sure. My gracious! What in the world? Oh, that's just dandy! Three horses running loose across the highway. The burn probably scared them. What if I hadn't been going as slowly as I am? I could have hit those horses, killing them, and probably killing me, too. The Forest Service could get sued for this crazy idea of theirs." And on and on I waxed for about 10 more miles.

Finally, I was out of the burn area and the smoke cleared. When I could go normal speed again, I thought about the lesson in this. The Forest Service knows what they're doing. They've been doing this for years. It's obvious the forest needed to be cleaned out. What if it was never done and someone accidentally lit a match? Then the entire surrounding forest would go up in smoke. So I'd been complaining about what was surely a wise plan.

I reflected on what God had done in my life. He had to light a fire to clean out the debris in my spirit. It was painful while it was burning. Sometimes more than painful; sometimes agonizing. The more blackness in the depths of my spirit, the hotter the fire had to be, and the longer it smoldered afterward.

No, I'm not saying God is sadistic. And, no, I'm not claiming that all suffering is to teach people lessons. But God knows far better than we do about a "controlled burn."

And like the black smoke of the forest fire, it was difficult to see what was going on when I was in the midst of it. Sometimes it felt as if I was running into horses and that I'd be killed. But it had to be done. I needed to remember the burn was a "controlled burn." In my life, the fire allowed me the opportunity to be fresh and new again by burning up the old. And the ashes—the lessons—will act as fertilizer for the new growth.

Could the curse of the blackness ultimately be transformed into one of God's greatest tools to teach me what I need to know, must know, to live the life abundant—

the life He has planned for me?

Yes, it could.

Yes, it has.

And, yes, it will.

Hammering the Gold

Heat was used to burn up the old in my life and employed to ferret out the gold. I was compelled to come face to face with the origins of my fears and my feelings of unworthiness.

While at Alpha, I learned that premature forgiveness can short-circuit the recovery process. The forgiveness must be at the conclusion of the enlightenment process, not at the launching. I needed the season of the rain: the heart-to-mind encounter with the damage inflicted on my fragile spirit.

After I walked the arduous journey of understanding, what, then, was I to do with the ones who had harmed and hurt me?

It was time to move ahead, to press onward, to strive for the gold. And, in this propelling, I made a decision to forgive those who had caused me turmoil and anguish. Without forgiveness, complete healing is not possible.

Forgiving does **not** denote forgetting. Often those who admonish us to forgive and forget want us to imagine that the pain didn't happen. God is the only one who can choose to forget. My torment will always be a part of me, but now I see my perpetrators as fallible, human beings—as are we all—locked in their own ways of "doing" rather than "being."

In an ancient Jewish document called the *Testaments of the Twelve Patriarchs* lies this wisdom: "If a man sin against thee . . . if he repent and confess . . . forgive him. . . . But if he be shameless, and persisteth in his wrongdoing even so forgive him for the heart, and leave to God the avenging."

God commands us to forgive as we have been forgiven. For now I can do no more, but I must do no less!

When one forgives, the captive is set free. I discovered the ensnared one, subconsciously yearning to be released, was **me.**

Makav: the Hammer

After the intense heat came a process of hammering to make the gold useful. Lustrous gold leaf is made from melted gold which subsequently goes through degrees of hammering. The first hammering is done with a hammer that weighs as much as 17 pounds; then a 10 pound hammer is used. And, finally, a 7 pound hammer finishes the process. This hammering produces sheets so thin that light shines through them, perhaps the golden light of the rainbow.

His name means blow of the hammer: Hammerschlag, a German-Jewish name. It is a translation of the Hebrew word *makav* which means the hammer. And that's precisely what Dr. Hammerschlag did. He relentlessly hammered me; he hammered to break up the frozenness in my spirit. Dr. H. had hammers of all shapes and sizes in his repair shop: standard hammers, tiny, precise rock hammers, and formidable jack hammers. He knew how, when, and where to use these hammers. He used them well.

Golden Opportunities

I am hopeful that through reading this material and absorbing the concepts, you are making more choices that foster healing and growth. You don't have to be a victim. Unfortunately, many golden opportunities are lost because of fear! When you think you have two choices—and neither one is good—allow God and your heart to guide you to a third or fourth or fifth alternative that may be much better for you. Take action that suits you when it contributes to keeping your head, mouth, and heart in a straight alignment. What others demand that you do, or insinuate is right, may have little to do with YOUR reality.

Finding the Gold

"Just gimme that gold!" you and I will no longer demand. "Going for the gold" means simply—and yet profoundly—finding joy in the journey.

We're walking in the rain and rejoicing in it, too. We're remembering that today will be golden if we choose to make it so.

Gold is pure, pristine.

Gold is the standard by which certain substances and currencies are judged.

Gold is a precious treasure.

Gold is what's right before our eyes, day in and day out; it's there all the time. All we have to do is be willing to look and see in a whole, new way. Tested by fire, separated from the dross, the glimmering, shimmering, breathtaking, magnificent gold.

My gold was discovered in the gift of life and the gifts of love: my family, my teachers, my friends, my Lord.

GOLD is:

My husband, Jim, who walked through the storm with me and only one time (that I know of) said, "I don't know how much more of this I can stand."

My children who said, "We don't know how to help you, Mom, but we're here for you."

My daughters-in-law who love my sons and delight my heart.

My granddaughters who bring me immeasurable joy.

Mom who taught me the value of hard work; who took me to church so that I could learn about JESUS.

Dad who let me ride behind him on the horse going very fast.

My brother, Ken, and sister, Vicki, who know from where I come.

Grandma Anderson who loved me beyond measure; who sustained and protected me and who helped save my life.

Aunt Luella and Uncle Sonny who modeled parenthood.

Mom Teilborg who loved and accepted me.

Dad Teilborg who is the father of my beloved husband.

My brother-in-law, Rich, and sister-in-law, Judy, who encouraged me by helping me to understand my aching heart and by listening, thoughtfully, to my pain.

My friends whom I won't list; who don't care

about being named anyway because that's the kind of friends you are. You're the ones who listened, ad nauseam, to the pain in my heart knowing you were powerless to do anything about it. You're the ones who came and sat with me when I was curled up in a tight, little ball. You're the ones who know me, through and through, and love me anyway. You're the ones who encourage me to just "be."

Dr. Alan Abromovich who led me to—

Dr. Andrew Weil who led me to—

Dr. Carl Hammerschlag.

Diana, my gifted friend and editor, who honed the manuscript with wisdom and severe mercy.

The Body of Believers at Open Door Fellowship who know about grace and mercy and courage, and, most of all, unconditional love.

Alpha Care with the bravery to do the noble; who stood against a myriad of critical spirits in order to provide a safe haven for women who have been bruised, battered, bludgeoned, and scarred by the storms of life.

Sam who has the willingness to show up every day for work on his new blue bike and who taught me important life lessons.

Brian and Melissa who showed me a whole new way to love.

Those who will always be in mental hospitals. May there be joy somehow, someway, for you on your journey.

The families and loved ones of those who couldn't keep-on-keeping-on; who took their own lives because they didn't understand there was any other way. May God grant you peace.

And, finally, those of you who have struggled with and are continuing to struggle with chronic or acute depression, or both. I have your pain in my heart. We are kindred spirits!

EPILOGUE
Revel in the Rainbow

One of my favorite stories as a child chronicled the journey of a little lady, her animals, and their quest for the perfect house. It's a tale of missing the rainbow.

Little Lady lived with her dog and cat in a cozy little house in the woods. Her lovely garden brought her joy. Horse was satisfied with the luscious grass in the pasture, Dog with the abundance of rabbits to chase in the meadow, and Cat with the toasty, warm hearth to nap on peacefully. Then a sad thing happened. Little Lady began pondering all the things her house **didn't** have; her mind obsessed on all she was missing. In fairly short order, she stopped cleaning the house and tending the garden. Predictably, one thing led to another and the outside of her home fell into disrepair.

Then one dreary day Little Lady noticed her home was looking dilapidated and that didn't please her or the animals. "We'd better move," they all said in unison. So . . . Little Lady loaded her belongings into her cart, hitched Horse to it, and off she went with Dog and Cat riding beside her looking for a new home.

"Ah! Here's a delightful house," Little Lady remarked as she unhitched the horse and moved her belongings inside. But pretty soon Horse complained there was insufficient pasture grass for him. "Not good," said Little Lady and she packed up everything and headed on down the road.

Eventually, she and the animals came to another house. "Doesn't this look to be a livable home?" she questioned her animals. At first blush it did, and Horse assured them there was plenty of grass. In they moved. Not many days passed before Dog complained there weren't rabbits to chase. They packed up once again.

Meanwhile, as this moving in and out business was going on, Painter was passing by Little Lady's abandoned place on his stroll home from work. "That's a nice house; all it needs is some paint and because I have extra, I'll paint it."

"There!" he remarked with a satisfied sigh as he completed the job. And on his merry way he went.

Returning from a trek to the flower farm, Gardener was hurrying along the road next to the deserted home of Little Lady. He noted that Little Lady's once carefully tended garden was overgrown with weeds. *I hate to see this garden looking so shabby; I wonder if that dear woman's been ill?* he thought to himself. *Perhaps I should do her a good turn and weed and plant her garden.* And, not only did he accomplish that task, he planted vibrant red geraniums in the window boxes and soft violets in the flowerpots by the door.

Presently, Maid from the big house up the road ambled by toting a big bag of fresh, sweet oranges. "Hello, Gardener. How are you today?"

"I'm fine, but you should have seen this garden. It was a disaster!"

"It certainly looks tidy now," affirmed Maid. "But if it was unkept, I'll bet the inside of the house is in shambles. I'll go check."

"My, oh my, what a mess!" she exclaimed. "Even though it's been recently painted, the rest of it certainly needs a woman's touch. I suppose I have time to spruce it up a bit." As she was leaving, exhausted but pleased, she left some oranges on the front step for anyone in need of refreshment.

Little Lady and the animals were still searching for the perfect house. "How about this one?" she questioned hopefully as she spotted yet another house. Cautiously, Horse approved the pasture and Dog had already found rabbits to chase. In they moved. But all too soon Cat announced, "This doesn't have a nice hearth for me to sleep by. I don't like this house!"

Discouragement set in for the animals as they wearily traveled on. "Let's not lose hope," encouraged Little Lady. "Surely we'll find the right and perfect house." As she was exhorting her animals, round the bend they went and there, nestled in a serene meadow, was a delightful, charming house.

"Glory me!" Little Lady clapped her hands. "Just exactly the house we've been searching for. Oh! Pretty RED geraniums in the window boxes and delicious-looking ORANGES on the front step. And YELLOW homes always look warm and inviting."

"O.K. by me," decided Horse. "Plenty of GREEN grass." Little Lady walked through the front door and was overjoyed when she saw the walls inside.

"Robin egg BLUE: my favorite color," she exclaimed. She gazed at the just setting sun as she went outside to get Cat. "Animals, do come and look at the gorgeous sunset," she implored.

"Sure is a pretty INDIGO sky," Dog panted as he ran off again. "Evening is a good time to chase rabbits, and I've seen plenty of them." When Little Lady and Cat turned to go in, Cat declared, "Look at these beautiful VIOLETS. I just adore velvety, soft violets." Once inside, Lady and Cat toured the rooms, and Cat claimed the hearth as her own—an ideal place to curl up and sleep.

Optimistically, Little Lady went out to unhitch Horse and that's when she noted the garden at the side of the house. "A glorious garden, Horse and Dog, and well taken care of, too. What luck!"

Later that evening as the animals settled down for a tranquil night's sleep, Little Lady relaxed by the fire to read her new book: *When You Miss the Rainbow.* Suddenly she got goosebumps. "Hmmm.... There's something strangely familiar about this house." She put the captivating book down, got up, and thoroughly inspected her new home from top to bottom.

"Oh, what a foolish Little Lady I am," she declared. "My home! This is the house I didn't appreciate, the one I neglected. To think, here it was all the time. It's truly the perfect home for us. And it's not an ordinary house."

"It's a golden home with golden opportunities!"

A Golden Afternoon

On a lazy, tranquil afternoon I sat on the front steps of our cabin in the woods. There was no sound but the chirping of birds and the banter of the squirrels as they chased one another to and fro. The multi-colored flowers looked lovely as they displayed their rainbow colors.

I sat quietly in the stillness and remembered.

I remembered the day I saw the rainbow—the day I knew I was to tell you my story.

I remembered: red, orange, yellow, green, blue, indigo, and violet.

Grieg's *"Morning"* from *The Peer Gynt Suite* was playing in the background.

I remembered standing in the doorway to the barn with my dad and Uncle Sonny. The ominous, black, hail cloud had blown by and in its place, gentle rain had come. We hoped for a good harvest. The horses and cattle had been fed, cows milked, and the sweet corn was nearly ripe. Uncle Sonny looked up at the sky and pointed to the glorious, perfect rainbow. Then he extolled with joy, “It just ‘don’t’ get much better than this!” It doesn’t, indeed.

So . . . let us ***REVEL IN THE RAINBOW***!